A2

CriticalThinking
for OCR

Tony McCabe • Jacquie Thwaites

www.heinemann.co.uk
✓ Free online support
✓ Useful weblinks
✓ 24 hour online ordering

01865 888058

Heinemann

Inspiring generations

Heinemann Educational Publishers
Halley Court, Jordan Hill, Oxford OX2 8EJ
Part of Harcourt Education

Heinemann is the registered trademark of Harcourt Education Limited

©Harcourt Education 2006

First published 2006

10 09 08 07 06
10 9 8 7 6 5 4 3 2 1

British Library Cataloguing in Publication Data is available
from the British Library on request.

10-digit ISBN: 0 435235826
13-digit ISBN: 978 0 435235 82 6

Typeset by Macmillan India Ltd.

Printed and bound in the UK by Ashford Colour Press, Gosport, Hants

Cover photo: M.C. Escher's "E61" © 2005 The M.C. Escher Company-Holland.
All rights reserved.

Acknowledgements
Every effort has been made to contact copyright holders of material reproduced in
this book, and to ensure information is correct at the time of printing. However,
the publisher will be pleased to rectify any omissions in subsequent printings if
notice is given.

The authors and publisher would like to thank the following individuals and
organisations for permission to reproduce photographs: pp 7, Photolibrary; pp 9,
Photofusion Picture Library/Alamy; pp 71, National Archives and Records
Administration; pp 74, Corbis.

We would like to thank the Office of National Statistics for permission to reproduce
the data on page 20, reproduced under the terms of the Click-Use Licence.

We would like to thank the following people for permission to reproduce
copyrighted material: pp 9, 12 and 84–85, The BBC; pp 34, (article from The
Observer) Copyright Guardian Newspapers Limited 2006; pp 34, (article from The
Guardian) Copyright Guardian Newspapers Limited 2006; pp 49, The Daily
Telegraph; pp 85, The Daily Mirror; pp 85, © The Independent, 11 August 2005.

Contents

Critical Thinking at A2 is both the same as at AS Level and different from it. There is an obvious and necessary sense of continuity: you will still be using the skills and language acquired in your AS modules. You will still be assessed on your ability to:

- analyse critically the use of different kinds of reasoning in a wide range of contexts (AO1)
- evaluate critically the use of different kinds of reasoning in a wide range of contexts (AO2)
- develop and communicate relevant and coherent arguments clearly and accurately in a concise and logical manner (AO3).

However, you will find that both of the A2 modules will be more challenging because:

- the arguments and evidence will be more complex
- you will explore more deeply the concepts, issues and problems involved
- some of the reasoning will be more complex and is likely to require a more focused approach from you and greater powers of concentration
- you will need to use and understand a greater range of specialist language at this higher level of Critical Thinking.

Assessment at A2 Critical Thinking will consist of two examinations:

- **Unit 3: Resolution of Dilemmas**. This is a written paper of 1 hour and 15 minutes and will account for 40% of the marks at A2. The structured questions are based on an issue or topic, about which evidence will be provided in the form of a Resource Booklet. You are also required to produce a piece of extended writing. You should attempt **all** questions. Approximately half of the marks for this unit will be allocated on the basis of how well you develop and communicate your arguments.

- **Unit 4: Critical Reasoning**. This paper will consist of 20 multiple-choice questions and structured questions set on longer passages. You will also have to produce a piece of extended writing in response to an extended stimulus passage. Again, you need to attempt **all** the questions. The paper lasts 1 hour and 45 minutes and will account for 60% of the marks at A2.

You can find full details in the OCR specification, available at www.ocr.org.uk. There are Heinemann textbooks covering Units 1, 2 and 4.

Introduction to Unit 3

Unit 3 – making decisions

You should see Unit 3 as a decision-making unit. It takes you through a process, from identifying a problem all the way to arriving at a solution. Unit 3 gives you the opportunity to develop and use your advanced skills in the context of issues that are topical, interesting and involving.

There will be fewer questions in the Unit 3 exam than in the other Critical Thinking exams. The questions will require you to:

- analyse and evaluate evidence provided in a Resource Booklet
- use relevant **criteria** to evaluate choices
- identify and explain a **dilemma** arising from the issue covered in the Resource Booklet
- write an argument which attempts to resolve the dilemma you have identified. In this argument you will be required to identify and apply **principles** to help you resolve the dilemma.

How will this book help me to cover Unit 3?

The first four chapters follow the pattern of the Unit 3 exam, as follows:

Chapter 1: Dealing with evidence

This chapter will explain how to:

- identify and deal with problems of definition often associated with evidence. For instance, we hear a lot about *terrorism*, but there may well be problems when it comes to actually defining what is meant by the term 'terrorism'
- use evidence to explain factors that might affect how we view different issues.

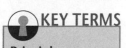

Chapter 2: Choices and criteria

This chapter will help you to understand more clearly what we mean by criteria and how we need to select and apply the appropriate criteria when considering a course of action in response to a problem.

Chapter 3: Identifying and defining dilemmas

This chapter will:

- examine in more detail what we mean when we talk in terms of a dilemma
- identify dilemmas arising from various situations
- demonstrate how to set out, or explain, a dilemma.

Chapter 4: The resolution of dilemmas – applying principles

This chapter will:

- identify and explain what we mean by principles
- help you to understand how the application of principles to a dilemma might help us to resolve it
- look at some ethical principles that might provide us with guidance in resolving a dilemma.

Chapter 5: Preparing for the exam

This chapter will explain the exam paper and the thinking behind it: what it will be asking you to do and what the examiner will be looking for in your answers. This will be very useful to you in terms of helping to improve your exam performance.

Chapter 6: Guidance to the activities

This chapter provides sample answers to the activities in Chapters 1–4.

Dealing with evidence

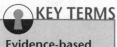

Unit 3 is about using Critical Thinking skills in the context of decision-making. We are going to take an **evidence-based approach** to help us through this process.

In the Unit 3 exam you will be required to:

- examine evidence provided on a particular issue in a critical and focused manner
- use criteria to evaluate choices related to this issue (this task will require you to refer closely to the evidence provided)
- develop and communicate an argument which deals with a dilemma arising from the issue under discussion.

Using evidence in Unit 3

Throughout Unit 3 you are required to use evidence in a critical and constructive manner. You need to be able to analyse and to evaluate various types of evidence with some considerable skill, avoiding comments which are vague and over-generalised.

- At this stage it is important that you see the close links between Unit 3 and the three other units that make up Critical Thinking A Level. You will be aware from Units 1, 2 and 4 of the importance that Critical Thinking places upon the use and evaluation of evidence.
- In this chapter you should be aware that we are following on from Units 1 and 2, particularly in terms of evaluating evidence.
- We will be using a broad range of evidence including data, figures, graphs, surveys and the opinions of expert witnesses and other interested parties, such as government ministers, religious leaders, commentators and pressure groups.
- When using evidence, for whatever purpose, we need to consider how useful it is for that purpose. Our aim throughout this unit is to use evidence to help us in the decision-making process. Establishing how useful evidence might be involves us in asking the right sort of questions of it. In other words, we need to interrogate our evidence.

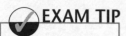 **EXAM TIP**

- In the exam you will be provided with a separate Resource Booklet which will contain up to four or five documents. It is very likely that these documents will contain a variety of different types of the evidence listed on page 5, for example, statistical/numerical evidence in the form of graphs, tables, charts; statements of policy; opinions; explanations.

 REMEMBER

Critical Thinking is not primarily a content-based subject. This means that you will not be required to have any in-depth knowledge of the actual topic covered by the evidence in the Resource Booklet. It is what you do with the evidence that is important.

What Chapter 1 covers

In this chapter you will learn how to:

- demonstrate that you are critically aware of problems of *definition and implementation*. We need to be aware of problems posed by *ambiguity* and *context*: how words and phrases and descriptions can sometimes carry all kinds of meaning and different connotations (see pages 7–12), and how crucially important differences in meaning can be when we come to make decisions

- use evidence provided to identify and explain relevant factors that might affect the way people view the issue under discussion. For example, people's ideas might be influenced by their religion or where they live.

Problems of definition and implementation

We are going to examine some sources of information on different topics in order to:

- identify possible problems when defining and using certain words/phrases in a particular context

- explain how and why these problems might arise

- assess the extent to which such problems might present difficulties when deciding on how best to respond to an issue.

WORKED EXERCISE: BULLYING IN SCHOOLS

Read this short passage and then look at the questions and comments that follow.

When surveyed, most schools stated that they took incidences of bullying very seriously. A high proportion of schools are either currently reviewing their policies or reviewing them annually.

One school made the comment that, due to the rapidly changing forms in which bullying is happening, for example the use of modern technology like the Internet, they review their policy every 6 months to keep pace with the changing environment.

In view of these rapidly changing forms of bullying, this practice of regular reviews of policy is worth sharing with other professionals.

1. Working on your own, attempt to write a brief definition of what constitutes bullying.

2. Compare your definition with others in your group. Can you as a group now decide on a common definition of bullying?

Comment

We could try to define what bullying is in two ways:

- By means of a short and inclusive statement, such as: *The inappropriate use of power.*

- By producing a list of what constitutes acts of bullying, such as: *Bullying is any activity that involves the following: deliberate aggression; inflicting pain and distress; the use of unequal power relationships; the persistent use of such activity/behaviour.*

Both of these attempts at definition can often be found in school handbooks. And both illustrate some problems we face when trying to define what is a very commonly used word – bullying.

3. Identify and explain what some of the problems with these definitions might be.

Comment

- The first definition – *the inappropriate use of power* – contains within itself problems of definition, such as:

  ○ A lack of clarity or precision as to what is meant by *inappropriate.* Is there some scale or measurement of behaviour that will enable us to judge what is and is not inappropriate?

  ○ An action which might be viewed as an inappropriate use of power by a child in a school environment may be viewed as appropriate if carried out by a teacher – such as making somebody sit next to someone they do not want to sit next to.

  ○ A similar kind of problem can occur when dealing with the sensitive issue of how far we should allow parents to go in dealing with their child's misbehaviour: where does discipline end and abuse begin?

- The second attempt at defining bullying could be said to be a description and not a definition as such. A particular problem with a list like this is it fails to define its terms: what, for example, does *persistent* mean?

- Both definitions could be viewed as over-influenced by things such as 'political correctness', 'liberalism' or the 'nanny state'. (Each of these terms, of course, poses in itself an issue of definition.)

> **4. One school refers to the use of modern technology like the Internet as representing a new form of bullying. How might this affect any policy we might draw up to deal with bullying?**

Comment

What we can see at work here is how change – cultural, economic, political or technological – can affect the way we define behaviour. Such changes can in turn affect how we might respond to a problem. In the case of bullying, we might well decide that to be fully effective any anti-bullying policy has to go beyond just looking at what can be done during school hours. For example, we might want to ask parents to regulate their child's access to the Internet. It becomes in this sense part of the debate about policing the World Wide Web.

WORKED EXERCISE: ANIMAL RIGHTS PROTESTERS

Read the following extract from a BBC news story.

Animal rights extremists were blamed when a building contractor pulled out of work on a controversial animal rights research centre for Oxford University after shareholders received threatening letters leading to a temporary drop in the company's share prices.

But Oxford University officials say they remain committed to building the £18 million project which will see mice, amphibians and monkeys being used in the search for cures for conditions like leukaemia, Alzheimer's and asthma.

Research scientists reacted angrily to what they said was 'blatant terrorism' and the government promised to clamp down on 'internal terrorists' and give better protection to such companies.

Source: www.newsbbc.co.uk

1. Select two words from this passage which in your view might present us with problems of definition.

2. Choose one of these words and explain why you think it might present problems of definition.

3. Use the problems you have identified to explain how such problems of definition might in turn lead to problems for the government in dealing with animal rights protesters.

Comment

1. Two words which might present problems of definition include 'extremists' and 'terrorists/terrorism'.

2. The use of the word 'extremists' to describe any direct action group could give rise to a number of problems. A sample answer might make some of the following points:

    Extremist

    - The use of the word 'extremist' can be used to unduly influence public opinion against the views represented by animal rights protesters.

- There is perhaps an implication here that the views of the protesters are also somehow dangerous and marginal, whereas animal rights protesters might claim that it is the practice of animal experimentation that is extremist, and so that what they are doing is in fact quite reasonable.

- As there is no objective definition of the word extremist, actions must be viewed and judged in context. There are no defined boundaries of what is normal.

Terrorist

- 'Internal terrorist' implies that society as a whole is at serious risk of attack and injury.

- Terrorist here is being used in a fairly imprecise way: we would need to know more about what sort of threats are being made and if there is strong evidence of them being carried out or of any intention to carry them out.

- There could be a legal definition of what constitutes 'terrorism' that may be different from the one intended by the research scientists referred to in the news report.

- It might be that 'terrorists' are so defined because they represent unpopular/minority views or because they are threatening established/privileged groups such as shareholders, in which case 'terrorists' might not be an appropriate word to use.

- We could argue that, in the case of both words under discussion, it is in the interests of the building contractors and the shareholders to use words like these in order to present animal rights protesters in the worst possible light.

3. It is the duty of the state/government to protect its citizens when they are exposed to the actions/threats of others that might cause them harm. Therefore threats made by animal rights protesters call for a *response*.

   The problem, though, comes in deciding upon what is an appropriate level of response. This is a problem of *implementation*.

   - In modern society anyone described as 'extreme' or as a 'terrorist' is very likely to be viewed as a serious threat that needs to be acted against quickly and with some severity. However, should the threat posed by some animal rights protesters – 'internal terrorists' – be taken as seriously as that presented by international terrorism?

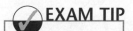

EXAM TIP

We have commented at some length here in order to show you that much can be said about problems of definition. You would not be required to make this number of points in the exam. Two relevant problems that are well developed should be enough to gain a very good mark.

- This might well be a matter of opinion, but there certainly appears to be an implication here in the use of these words that the same kind of measures should be taken against animal rights 'extremists' as are being taken against other forms of terrorism. The shareholders threatened or attacked may well demand of the government that it be consistent.

- It might, therefore, be difficult for the government – or security forces – to respond in a more low-key, and perhaps more appropriate manner, to any threat posed by animal rights protesters.

- An unduly severe reaction on the part of the security forces might run the risk of encouraging protesters to be more 'extreme' and to be more likely to commit acts of 'terrorism'.

- Labelling protesters as extremist/terrorists might make it more difficult for the government/the scientific establishment to respond rationally and fairly to what might be legitimate views held by opponents of animal experimentation.

A summary of problems of definition

Depending upon the issue you will be dealing with in the exam and upon the context in which the words/phrases occur, relevant problems could include:

- ambiguity in language and usage

- context: words and phrases can convey different meanings/messages depending upon social/political/cultural contexts

- different types of sources might define/use certain key words in different ways, each of which could well be acceptable in its own context, for example, scientific/non-scientific usage, legal/non-legal usage

- established/majority/common definitions/usage might not allow for minority views/interpretations, based perhaps on ethnic/religious/political perspectives

- there may be cases where certain key words are being used in such a way as to unfairly influence policy or public opinion, thus shaping the terms of debate.

ACTIVITY ❶

Read the following report from the BBC news website and then:

a) Explain in what ways the use of the word 'respect' here could present us with problems of definition.

b) Suggest some ways in which these problems of definition might lead to difficulties when it comes to implementing policies aimed at reducing anti-social behaviour in our communities.

> *Tony Blair's so-called 'respect agenda' emerged as a broad idea during the 2005 general election campaign. He said that it was about putting the law-abiding majority back in charge of their local communities:*
>
> *'Whether it is in the classroom, or on the streets in town centres on a Friday or Saturday night, I want to focus on this issue. We have done a lot so far with anti-social behaviour orders and additional numbers of police. I want to make this a particular priority for this government, how we bring back a proper sense of respect in our schools, in our communities, in our towns and villages.'*
>
> *ASBOs [Anti-Social Behaviour Orders] and extra numbers of police have been used to try to tackle bad behaviour and encourage people – particularly younger people – to be more respectful.*
>
> *Source: www.newsbbc.co.uk*

Using evidence to identify relevant factors

The evidence you will be dealing with in the exam will help you to identify the factors that might affect people's views on the issue you are exploring.

It will help if you think in terms of the different types of factors – or considerations or circumstances – that can influence the way we look at things. The way in which we react to an issue or to a suggested change in the way things are done is likely to be affected by a range of factors, such as:

- **economic** – money, business, employment, use of resources, trade, etc.
- **social/cultural** – family life, neighbourhoods, education, age, gender, attitudes, religion, background and so on.

- **morality/ethics** – what people think is right and wrong (this is linked to social/cultural, but worth considering on its own)
- **health and safety** – risks to people's physical and psychological well-being
- **political** – the government, the power of the state, elections, local government and international relations
- **legal** – what society permits and does not permit in a formal or legal sense; crime and punishment; international law
- **geographical/regional** – where you live might well be a factor in determining your response to issues such as conservation or house building for example
- **aesthetic considerations** – the appearance of things, such as buildings, the arts, public spaces, parks and so on.

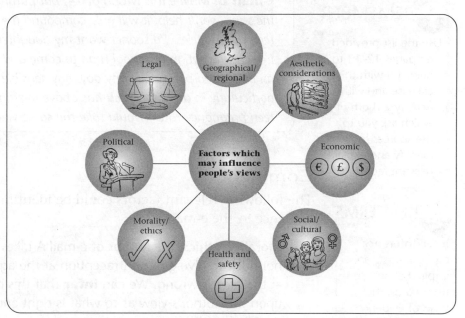

A spidergram on different types of factors that could influence people's views

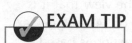

EXAM TIP

When you are asked to identify and explain a number of relevant factors, think about what kind of factors are most likely to be taken into account given the issues covered by the documents the question refers to. This should save you time by pointing you in the right direction.

You may think that there is a great deal of overlap between these factors, and this is true. But it will help you to think of relevant factors if you have a classification system like this in your mind. It is likely that certain sets of factors will be more relevant than others, depending upon the issue you are looking at.

For instance, take the issue of teenage pregnancy. It is likely that factors connected with this issue are going to be those most associated with categories such as morality/ethics and economic, social/cultural and health and safety issues. It is very unlikely that aesthetic considerations will play any part.

WORKED EXERCISE: THE PROBLEM OF TEEN MOTHERS

 EXAM TIP

Remember that you have to identify factors from a particular document or documents. You could pick a word or phrase from the document to show that you are using it.

REMEMBER

Use the list provided on pages 12–13 to help you with this exercise and with Activity 2 (both of which ask you to use sources to identify and explain relevant factors).

KEY TERMS

Infer/Inference – an *inference* is an implied conclusion reached on the basis of evidence and reasoning. In other words, it is something we have to work out from information and evidence we are given. Thus we can *infer* from what e-mail A is saying that the morning-after-pill should not be given to girls of a school age

Here we have two e-mails that were sent to a local newspaper in response to a story about a school that was considering offering the morning-after-pill to girls from the age of 14. Read them and then *identify and explain three factors* that might affect how the people who have written the e-mails react to the idea of giving contraception to girls below the age of 16.

> **E-mail A:** *This is wrong. Sex at 14 is wrong. I did not even know how to spell the word at 14, never mind anything else.*

> **E-mail B:** *Maybe it is wrong at 14, but putting our head in the sand won't help, it will only compound the problem of teen pregnancies. I'd sooner want my daughter to be receiving free contraception at school than to come and explain she has an unwanted pregnancy any day. Any sensible person, particularly in an area which has above average unwanted teen pregnancy rates, would take the same view.*

Comment

The following relevant factors could be identified using the evidence in the e-mails:

- **Morality/ethics:** the author of e-mail A takes the view that it is not right to give girls contraception at the age of 14 because sex at that age is wrong. We can **infer** that this reaction is based upon the author's view as to what is right and wrong from a moral – or ethical – perspective.

- **Legal:** we might also infer from the statement in e-mail A ('sex at 14 is wrong') that the author is referring to the fact that it is illegal to have sex below the age of 16. There is an interesting discussion to be had about whether the writer objects on legal or moral grounds or both.

 REMEMBER

We will be dealing with definitions and explanations of morality and ethics in more detail in Chapter 4. By the time you have completed Unit 3 you should feel confident in using a wide range of concepts and vocabulary associated with issues to do with the *rightness* or *wrongness* of an action.

- **Social/cultural** (generational attitudes): e-mail A uses his/her own experience as a 14-year-old to support their argument that sex at this age 'is wrong'. It is clear that their own upbringing is a significant factor in affecting how they react to the idea of giving the morning-after-pill to a 14-year-old.

- **Health and safety** (the well-being of the young person): While e-mail B acknowledges that 'it may be wrong' to provide a 14-year-old girl with contraception in this way, the main factor the author takes into account is the effect an 'unwanted' pregnancy is likely to have on the 14-year-old.

- **Geographical/regional:** e-mail B refers to the area as having above average teen pregnancy rates. Living in such an area might be a significant factor in raising awareness of the problem of the issue of teen pregnancies. The coverage of the issue by the local media suggests this to be the case.

Looking forward

Unit 3 is entitled *Resolution of Dilemmas.* Later on in this book, particularly in Chapters 3 and 4, we will be examining **dilemmas**, looking at how we might try to resolve them in some detail. But you should already be thinking in terms of *identifying* dilemmas.

Remember that a dilemma occurs where you have to make a difficult choice between two courses of action, both of which have some negative consequences.

In the case of the morning-after-pill we could express the dilemma in the following way:

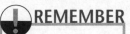
REMEMBER

Remember a **dilemma** is a situation where a choice has to be made between two conflicting options, each of which will result in some undesirable consequences.

> *Do we provide the morning-after-pill in schools even though it might encourage under-age sex with all the problems that can bring in terms of health and parental disapproval; or do we decide not to provide it and run the risk of a rise in under-age pregnancies with all the unfavourable consequences which would follow?*

It will be good practice for you to get into the habit early on of analysing situations in these terms. You could, for instance, do the same with the issue of animal rights.

ACTIVITY

In this activity you need to use evidence to help in identifying and explaining relevant factors. Documents A and B below are about the differences between what men and women are paid. This is referred to as the 'gender pay gap'.

Study these documents carefully and then identify and explain three factors that might affect people's views on the gender pay gap.

In your answer you should:

- clearly identify each relevant factor by referring to the document(s)

- ensure that you include a brief explanation with each factor. For example, it is not enough to just say 'a moral factor'; you will need to develop your answer, as is indicated in the example on teenage pregnancies (see pages 14–15).

Document A: Extracts from the Women and Work Commission Report, February 2006

- Female workers suffer one of the biggest gender pay gaps in Europe – 17 per cent for full-time staff and 38 per cent for part-time staff – because they are more likely to be in low paid jobs and then slip down the career ladder after having children.

- Lady Prosser, the Chairwoman of the Commission, said that *'Many women are working, day in day out, far below their abilities. This waste of talent is an outrage.'*

- Recommendations of the Report were that the government should:

  - take action to tackle gender stereotypes

  - encourage skilled part-time jobs

  - support women returning to work

  - extend flexible working rights to parents of older children

  - provide £5 million to train trade union equality representatives to monitor pay.

Document B: Some reactions to the Women and Work Commission Report

- **Katherine Rake**, Director of the Fawcett Society (an organisation that campaigns for equal opportunities for women)

  'This report has short-changed a generation of women. If this government wants to go down in history as having closed the pay gap, it is going to have to try a lot harder. The time is long due for vigorous measures.'

- **John Gridland**, Deputy Director of the CBI (the Confederation of British Industry – an organisation representing employers)

  'I was staggered at how poor career guidance and education has become; we are failing a whole generation of young people – essentially young girls.'

- **George Osbourne**, the Shadow Chancellor of the Exchequer (speaks for the opposition party in the House of Commons; a leading member of the Conservative Party)

  'In the past, Conservatives have given the impression that young mothers should stay at home. Today, the Labour Party gives the impression that all young mothers should work. Both are wrong…We should support the choice that young mothers make for themselves.'

SUMMARY

This chapter has helped you to:

- use evidence to demonstrate your awareness that how we might define certain key words and phrases can be problematic
- explain how such problems of definition can, in turn, make it more difficult to devise and implement policies
- use evidence in identifying factors that might affect how people view a range of issues.

In Chapter 1 we examined evidence for two particular purposes:

- To explore problems of definition.
- To help us to identify and explain factors that influence how people react to certain issues or problems.

In Chapter 2 you will:

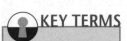

KEY TERMS

Choices – here we are referring to the different options that might be available to us when we are responding to situations where decisions need to be made. The government or other organisations might refer to these options as policies or strategies

- examine how we use evidence critically to help us identify what might be appropriate **choices** in response to issues of concern
- examine how we need to develop and assess the relevance of **criteria** to enable us to decide upon a course of action
- use criteria we have identified, in the context of the evidence provided, to evaluate the choices made.

Using evidence to identify possible choices

Here we could talk in terms of *framing* choices or policy alternatives. Whether we are deciding upon which university to apply to or what to do about nuclear energy, the process is more or less the same.

KEY TERMS

Criteria – the plural of **criterion**, which is a standard by which something may be judged or decided. For example, *organic foodstuff must meet the criterion of being free of chemicals in its production*

It is likely that we will start off with at least some sort of a view about the problem or issue. We might even think that we know straight away what should or should not be done. However, this is where we might need to be very careful not to base our decisions on emotion or prejudice.

Think in terms of some of the issues looked at in Chapter 1:

- anti-social behaviour
- teenage pregnancy
- the gender pay gap.

KEY TERMS

Collective – refers to situations where groups of people are affected as a whole rather than just on an individual level. **Collective decisions** are those made by, or on behalf of, society or institutions as a whole

Each of these issues is the subject of much analysis and debate. All three are of concern to us, both on an individual and **collective** level.

It follows, then, that responses to each of these issues – and to any number of other problems – are likely to involve us acting collectively. This may well mean government intervention, for example, via the police and the courts. Decisions have to be made: what to do; what not to do; what policies to put in place; how effective are such policies likely to be? Before reaching decisions we need to examine relevant evidence.

Assessing what the evidence tells us

REMEMBER

In Units 2 and 4 you will have developed – or will be developing – the Critical Thinking skills involved in evaluating a range of different types of evidence. Unit 3 is very much concerned with applying these skills in the context of making decisions.

It is very likely that using evidence to help us choose the best course of action, in relation to the sort of issues we are looking at here, is going to be problematic.

WORKED EXERCISE: THE GENDER PAY GAP REVISITED

In Chapter 1 we looked at responses to the differences between what men and women are paid. One of the factors you might well have identified is education – the CBI referred to '*poor career guidance and education ... essentially [that of] young girls*'.

Study the evidence on page 20 provided by the Women's Equality Unit of the Office of National Statistics.

Suggest some problems you think might arise in using this evidence to support the choice to invest more in career guidance and education for girls, in order to help close the gender pay gap.

The job gap – occupational segregation in Britain, percentages

Occupations	% women	% men
Receptionists	95	5
Nurses	88	12
Primary and nursery teachers	87	13
Cleaners and domestics	80	20
Retails cashiers and check-out operators	77	23
Office managers	67	33
Retail and wholesale managers	35	65
Marketing and sales managers	26	74
Software professionals	17	83

Source: The Women's Equality Unit of the Office of National Statistics

Comment

While this evidence is relevant to the issue of unequal pay and could be of some use in suggesting there is a link between education and lower pay, we must be careful not to base reasoning upon an over-simplistic, and therefore flawed, view of cause and effect. Some of the problems with using the evidence to support the choice might therefore include:

- The evidence only gives us information about the types of job which are more or less likely to be occupied by women. We might assume from this that most of the occupations the majority of women are employed in are lower paid, and in turn infer that this could be a major factor in women earning less (the gender pay gap), but it is important to recognise that this particular piece of evidence does not, in itself, prove this to be the case.

- Also the figures in themselves do not explain *why* women are more represented in some occupations than in others. To support the choice to invest more in career guidance and education for girls we would need to establish a link between deficiencies in education or poor career guidance and women occupying the majority of lower paid professions but the evidence does not provide this link.

- There are also other important factors which could explain why women might occupy the majority of lower paid occupations, rather than deficiencies in education or poor career guidance. For example some of these lower paid occupations might allow women to work more 'children-friendly' hours. (Although you could still argue that the problem is education in its broadest sense, i.e. society's expectations of who should bear the primary responsibility for looking after children.)

- Trying to establish a link between deficiencies in education and women occupying the majority of lower paid occupations is also likely to be problematic because some of the occupations in which women dominate, such as Primary school teaching, require higher level educational qualifications. Neither can nursing be viewed as unskilled in any way.

ACTIVITY ③

 EXAM TIP

A question like this might be worth approximately six marks in an exam. If this is the case, be careful not to spend too much time on it. Clear, but brief, identification and explanation of roughly three relevant points will be enough.

What problems might arise in using the evidence provided below when assessing whether or not ASBOs should continue to play a significant role in combating anti-social behaviour?

ASBOs issued between 1999 and 2005

Area	Total number of ASBOs issued
Avon and Somerset	150
Cheshire	140
Devon and Cornwall	135
Greater London	670
Greater Manchester	938
Humberside	169
Merseyside	172
Nottinghamshire	173
West Midlands	485
Surrey	62
Total for England	6227
Wales – total	270

Source: www.crimereduction.gov.uk

Continued

Notes:

- In recent years, one of the most high-profile ways of trying to combat unruly and intimidating behaviour in local neighbourhoods has been to give the courts powers to issue ASBOs.

- Once issued against named individuals, ASBOs are then implemented by the police and local authorities. Names and photographs of those served with ASBOs are sometimes published in local newspapers. ASBOs are now very much part of the law and order scene.

We can see that using evidence to help us to choose the best course of action can be extremely problematic. This demonstrates how important it is to evaluate critically the relevance of such evidence.

Different types of choice

In the exam you may be presented with different types of choice. It may be helpful therefore, for us to clarify what different types of choice there might be, depending upon the problem being addressed. Some of the different types of choice you might be presented with may include the following:

- a range of options
- alternatives
- a continuum of choices.

A range of options

This is where we are presented with a number of different options and might select one or more, or all of them, depending largely on what our resources will permit us to do. For example, a school or college or a workplace might decide to improve the health of its personnel with a health promotion. A number of suggestions spring to mind – posters, education, healthy eating options on the menu, subsidies to encourage the use of the gym, sports halls and the like; even organised work-outs for all every morning. The option or options chosen might be determined as much by resources as anything else.

Alternatives

Here we are presented with options where we do have to choose between one or the other, for example, choosing which university you would like to attend; here you have to choose one university (once you have decided, of course, that you are going to go to university). You cannot go to more than one university at a time.

A continuum of choice

A continuum of choice involves us considering options of increasing intervention or severity. Take the case of responding to the gender pay gap. Here we might decide that the key thing is to encourage employers to employ more women in higher paid posts. In this case the following continuum represents a series of choices which could be made:

- Introduce a voluntary code of practice whereby employers agree to try to move towards employing a quota of women in higher paid posts.
- Introduce a compulsory scheme of quotas for women in higher paid positions, under which firms will be liable to fines if they do not comply.
- Introduce such a scheme where the penalty for non-compliance is imprisonment.

Criteria

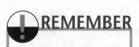

REMEMBER

In order to succeed in the Unit 3 exam, it is essential that you have a good understanding of the importance of using criteria in the decision-making process.

Before we decide on which course of action to take, we need to identify and explore relevant criteria. Criteria are the means by which you decide on a reasoned course of action.

The role and importance of criteria in making choices

Even in the most everyday situations where decisions are required we need to have some means of judging what might be our best course of action. For instance, when deciding where to go on holiday a family might apply a criterion based upon what facilities are available for the children. There will almost certainly be the criterion of cost to consider too.

We also need some way of assessing whether or not we have done the right thing. Decisions we make often require us to make further decisions in the future: 'should we continue doing what we originally decided to do?' is a fairly obvious one.

It is very important in all this that we select the criteria that are the most appropriate to the type of decision we are considering.

Identifying and developing relevant criteria

We need to be aware that there are different types of criteria. This is important to us in Unit 3 because there are likely to be different ways of testing whether or not criteria have been met.

Although distinctions between types of criteria cannot always be precise, one useful way of broadly categorising criteria is as follows:

- moral/ethical
- pragmatic
- political
- economic.

Moral/ethical

Moral (or ethical) criteria are concerned with right and wrong behaviour and the goodness or badness of the actions of individuals or groups. Under this heading we would include criteria concerned with considerations such as: *fairness; equality; harm.*

Pragmatic

A pragmatic approach to decision-making involves trying to deal with a problem and making choices in a way that is based on practical rather than theoretical considerations. If you are being pragmatic you will try to be realistic rather than idealistic. The sort of criteria here would include such considerations as: *effectiveness; efficiency; sustainability.*

Political

This is a word that can be used in a number of different ways, not all of them complimentary! Strictly speaking, it refers to the state, the government or the public affairs of the country. It is also used to refer to the ideas and activities of the various political parties. In a more derogatory sense, a decision might be described as *political* because it has an eye to what might prove popular and to what advantage there could be in it for an individual or a party. Political criteria are often also pragmatic and can include considerations such as: *public acceptability/will such a measure be popular?; does it fit in with party policy?; will our international allies approve?*

Economic

Economic factors are concerned with the use and distribution of resources. We will be using a fairly broad definition of economic criteria, which will include things such as employment, costs, the creation of wealth and its distribution, overseas trade, the local economy, government spending and taxation. We will consider, too, issues concerning the effective use of resources and value for money.

When we come to use criteria to help us to make choices, it is likely that we will aim for a range of different types of criteria. To help you do that, try the activity below.

ACTIVITY ④

Below is a list of different criteria that might usefully be applied in a wide range of decision-making situations. Your task is to arrange them into one or more of our main categories: *moral*, *pragmatic*, *political* and *economic*.

You can do this task in the form of a table, as indicated below. The first three have been done for you. You will notice that there is a question mark against one of the ticks. You may find that it is not always easy to decide which category some of the criteria belong to and this can stimulate discussion.

Criteria:

- Legality
- Public safety
- Sustainability
- Impact on the environment
- Value for money
- Personal freedom
- Equality of opportunity
- Impact on community relations
- Effects on wildlife
- Adherence to international norms and conventions.

Criteria	Moral	Pragmatic	Political	Economic
Legality	✓		✓	
Public safety	✓	✓ (?)	✓	
Sustainability		✓		✓

Another way of classifying criteria

If you attend a university admission or job interview, it is likely that the people interviewing you will have a criteria sheet in front of them. Most of these interview criteria sheets will have a number of qualities listed under two main headings:

- **Essential:** these will include things like qualifications, relevant experience and some personal qualities required for you to be able to take on the job/course.
- **Desirable:** these are likely to include further qualifications, a wider range of experience and the ability to start tomorrow.

Presumably, for you to be invited for interview, you must already be considered to fulfil most, if not all, of the criteria under the first heading. Criteria such as these could be taken to represent the limits within which you are operating at any given time in any given situation.

And just as there are limits placed upon your choices – such as lack of qualifications – there are limits placed upon firms and universities in terms of the choices open to them. There may not be enough really well-qualified candidates; there may be too many. In the first case, the criteria might have to be changed – some might have to be removed altogether. In the second case, more criteria might have to be introduced and/or existing ones tightened up.

We can use the classification of criteria on the interview sheet to produce a further classification of our own. In other words, as well as using the moral, pragmatic, political and economic classifications, we can arrange our criteria under the following headings:

- essential or highly relevant
- sufficient
- desirable.

We might feel that some criteria *have* to be fulfilled before we can choose to do something or before we can say something is right – that they are *essential* or *highly relevant* criteria. It seems unlikely, however, that there will be many decision-making situations in which there will be one criterion that is on its own *sufficient*. For this to be the case it would have to be considered enough on its own to justify the choice. For example, it is unlikely that cost on its own could be a sufficient criterion in deciding whether or not to

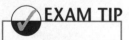
EXAM TIP

*When you are asked to use criteria to evaluate a chosen course of action you should place most emphasis on those criteria you feel are the most **relevant** in the context of the issue under discussion. Think in terms of essential criteria. It is unlikely that there will be a sufficient criterion.*

relocate a government department from London to Grimsby, as there are likely to be many other relevant criteria to take into account, for example infrastructure. It could well, however, be an essential criterion.

The final category in which we might place some of our criteria is that labelled *desirable*. This may seem a bit like saying, while we are at it, it would be nice if we could have that too, and in a way it is. But what if we have a situation where we need to choose between two possibilities and all the essential criteria are equally well met in both cases? In this case, it might be seen as useful to refer down our list to consider desirable criteria.

ACTIVITY 5

- Refer back to the list of criteria given for Activity 4 on page 25.

- Look at the following three issues, each of which throw up options for us to consider:

  ○ nuclear energy

  ○ smoking

  ○ public demonstrations, such as protest marches.

- From the list given in Activity 4, identify two criteria that are likely to play an important or necessary role in assessing policies in relation to each of the three issues.

- Explain why you have chosen each criterion.

Using criteria: identifying relevance and problems

For criteria to be applied effectively they should be:

- **readily understood** – your criteria ought to be clearly phrased

- **relevant** to the possible choices you have identified: there should be a good fit between the criterion and the situation under discussion. Some criteria are likely to be more appropriate in the evaluation of certain courses of action than others. Making a decision about whether we allow some form of euthanasia, for instance, is hopefully much more likely to involve ethical rather than economic considerations

- **measurable** where possible/appropriate.

You will need to bear these points closely in mind throughout the rest of this chapter.

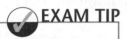
When considering a course of action we might ask some, or all, of the following questions (bearing in mind the classifications of moral, pragmatic, political and economic factors we have discussed earlier):

1. Should we do this because it is the *right* thing to do? For instance, will it involve people being treated equally?

2. Will it work?

3. Will it be popular?

4. Will it represent an effective use of resources?

These questions will, in effect, form the basis of our criteria (however we might choose to phrase them).

However, it is more than likely that any criterion we identify as being relevant and useful will also bring with it some problems of which we need to be aware.

WORKED EXERCISE: HANDLING ANTI-SOCIAL BEHAVIOUR

Consider using *public opinion* as a criterion in choosing how to respond to young people who display disruptive and disorderly behaviour.

Consider first these options:

- Increase the number of ASBOs handed out to young people.
- Impose more Dispersal Orders, which give the police powers to break up groups of people congregating in public places and to move them on.
- Impose a curfew on young people being out between certain hours.

We might choose one of these options, or we might adopt two of them or even all three: the criteria we decide to use might very well determine which option we take. We might, of course, decide to do none of these things, though this seems unlikely when we consider the growing strength of public opinion on this topic. The first two options require no additional powers. Imposing a curfew, however, would probably be seen as a more drastic action and would probably lead to considerable debate.

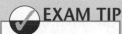**EXAM TIP**

You could get a question on the problems of using a particular criterion or on the relevance of a particular criterion in terms of making particular choices. Read the question very carefully and look at the number of marks before attempting it.

Whatever we choose to do, it is very likely that public opinion will play a part in our decision.

1. **What importance do you think should be attached to public opinion as a criterion in formulating a policy to deal with disruptive and disorderly behaviour amongst young people?**

Comment

Remember that we have already said that for a criterion to be of real use to us it should be:

- **readily understood:** a criterion should be relatively easy to understand and concisely phrased. Phrases such as *public opinion* or *public acceptability* are easily recognisable.

- **relevant:** does such a criterion fit? In other words, are the views and demands of the public likely to be a significant factor in influencing what is being decided here? We could argue that public support for a measure such as a curfew is vital because, without widespread support, it would be very difficult to enforce. Evidence we looked at earlier confirms that disorderly or anti-social behaviour amongst young people is an issue of public concern. (Over 6000 ASBOs were issued between 1999 and 2005.) The success or otherwise of any policies are very likely to have to be tested in terms of public acceptability.

- **measurable:** we do have a means of trying to assess what the public is thinking and what it might or might not be in favour of via surveys, opinion polls, meetings, consultations and so on.

It would appear, then, that using public opinion/acceptability as a criterion to help us to make choices in this context would be expected, appropriate and measurable and that, therefore, we should attach a great deal of importance to it.

However, we have to go on to ask the question below.

2. **What *problems* are likely to arise in using public opinion/acceptability as a criterion in deciding how to respond to anti-social behaviour in young people?**

KEY TERMS

Indicator – a measurement or means of showing the state or level of something. An indicator is used to show how an organisation is performing. For example, *the number of students gaining five or more GCSEs at grades A*–C is one* **indicator** *of how well a school is performing*. An indicator might also be used to demonstrate a trend, as in *a fall in the sale of crisps might* **indicate** *a trend towards more healthy eating habits*

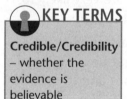

KEY TERMS

Credible/Credibility – whether the evidence is believable

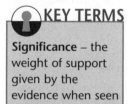

KEY TERMS

Significance – the weight of support given by the evidence when seen in the whole context

Comment

What we have to think about here is whether or not anything could be said *against* using public opinion as a criterion in helping us to make decisions about what to do about our unruly 15- and 16-year-olds. Is there an argument for being careful here?

There certainly is and it could include points such as:

- To use public acceptability as a criterion we need to be confident that we have **indicators** of public opinion that are *accurate, credible* and *representative*:

  ○ **Accurate:** because we need to be sure that the standards of statistical analysis and handling have clearly been applied (this is vital for any form of measurement to be of use). Raw data which shows what the public is thinking (gleaned from opinion polls or other forms of survey) must be handled with great care.

  ○ **Credible:** if we are using indicators to help us to make decisions we need to be reasonably confident that what they tell us is actually the case. For instance, we might look at a breakdown of the results of a survey that has been undertaken amongst the residents of an estate. The survey seeks to find out what the residents think should be done about gangs of teenagers who are causing a nuisance. This breakdown might be presented in the form of graphs, pie charts, bar charts, percentages, etc. and reflect the highest standards of statistical analysis. But we would still need to consider the following points:

    – What if people responding to the survey have misunderstood some of the questions or have responded to them without much thought?

    – What if the questions have not been sufficiently well targeted to provide the kind of information we need?

    – **Significance:** what if the results of such a survey might be different if opinions are canvassed at a different time of the year? For example, the summer holiday period can provoke a lot more complaints from older people about the behaviour of young people.

  ○ **Representative:** a variation of reliability, in that we want to be sure that the result of any survey shows us what a *range* of people are thinking. For example, even if you only want to know what the over-sixties feel about the idea of a curfew, you will still need to be sure that you have not just polled a particularly grumpy set of older people. You would want, of course, to ask a representative sample, based perhaps upon gender, family type, race or ethnic group, social class and so on. But, as a local authority or as a chief of police, you would not just want to look at the results of a survey that shows you only what the over-sixties think should be done with young people. You would want an indicator that at least represents a spread of age groups amongst other things.

- There is another serious problem that could arise from using public opinion as a criterion for action. This revolves around what happens if the public's view on what should be done might be considered in itself to be unacceptable – unacceptable, perhaps, on the basis of being extreme or discriminatory or impracticable. (Such a situation, interestingly for us, might well represent something of a dilemma.)

We have dealt at length with the application of one criterion in order to draw out some of the ways in which using criteria can cause problems as well as being helpful to us when it comes to making choices. You need now to see how well you can go through this process yourself.

ACTIVITY ❻

Look at the *effective use of resources* as a criterion. Show how we might use it to help us make choices when responding to anti-social behaviour. In doing so, remember that a criterion should be:

- **readily understood**
- **relevant**
- **measurable where possible/appropriate.**

What you need to do is:

a) Make a list of points to show how applying the criterion of 'effective use of resources' might help us to make a decision.

b) Make a list of potential problems that might arise in using such a criterion.

c) Explain the points you have noted and the problems you have identified to other members of the group. (You might be working in pairs, small groups or as a whole class, but the end result of the activity should be a record of the overall views of the group in an appropriate form.)

Using criteria to evaluate choices

In this final section of Chapter 2 we are going to bring together what we have been looking at in terms of *using evidence, framing choices* and *identifying relevant criteria*.

We will do this by using criteria and referring to evidence to evaluate possible choices that we have identified.

Examining a decision to impose a curfew on young people

How might we have reached a decision such as to impose a curfew on young people being on the streets between certain hours? We could have started by asking these two questions:

1. Will this work?

2. Will it cost much?

If, after considering relevant evidence, we decided that the answer was 'yes' to the first question and 'no' to the second, then our decision would seem to be a good one. It would certainly meet the pragmatic criterion of being an effective course of action. It would also appear to be an effective use of resources, thereby giving value for money and fulfilling our economic criterion.

But what if the answer is 'yes' to both questions? Then we have a more complicated situation on our hands. Some kind of balance has to be struck, just as one might need to strike a balance between the moral and the political. This, then, becomes a question of judgement: how far does the one criterion outweigh the other?

Finally, what if the answer is 'no' to the first question? In other words, we don't think the curfew will work. Does it then matter what the answer to the second question is?

To attempt to answer this we need to bring in a consideration of moral and political types of criteria. Consider the following scenario:

> *A suggested course of action is, after consideration, thought unlikely to have much effect. It might even prove to be quite costly. (Though why bother if it is not going to work, even if it is relatively cheap to implement?) Yet the government decides to go ahead with it anyway.*

On the face of it, this is something of a riddle. How might we solve it and explain the government's actions? We can do this by applying additional criteria to help us to evaluate the choice that has been made.

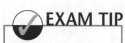

EXAM TIP

This process of balancing criteria against each other is one that you should familiarise yourself with. It will be particularly useful when you are attempting to resolve a dilemma.

REMEMBER

Everything you study in Unit 3 is about examining the decision-making process. As in the exam, one section leads on to another and the whole process is inter-linked.

Look again at the suggestion that we place a curfew on young people between, for example, the hours of 9 p.m. and 6 a.m. What happens if further research strongly suggests that such a policy just will not work because it will be unenforceable? What if, in addition, we are not too sure how much the curfew scheme is going to cost but nonetheless, we decide to go ahead with the scheme anyway?

How could we defend such a choice? Because we are stupid?

No, because we are smart, if somewhat unscrupulous, politicians. We have equally convincing evidence that such a curfew will be very popular with voters. As the voting age is 18, young people under that age will not be able to register their opinion in the polling booths anyway.

But also, on a less unworthy note, we might be convinced that, ineffective as it might be, a curfew is the *right* and *moral* thing to do. It is wrong for young people to be out after nine o'clock at night.

Therefore, if we consider it necessary to fulfil both political and moral criteria, choosing to impose a curfew might appear to be quite a reasonable step to take even if we are not sure that it will be effective.

Case study: Supermarkets

- Examine the following *evidence* about supermarkets (see Documents A, B and C).
- Examine the *choices* suggested.
- Examine the *criteria.*
- Then complete Activity 7 which follows.

Evidence

Document A: MPs declare war on power of the supermarket giants

MPs will demand a series of Draconian curbs on the power of the supermarkets in a hard-hitting report into the future of the high street. The report by the All-Party Parliamentary Small Shops Group will call for the Office of Fair Trading to trigger a full-blown investigation into the supermarket sector. Recommendations include:

- *an end to what MPs will say is the unfair advantage supermarkets derive from offering free car parking while shoppers wishing to use local stores have to pay to park on the high street*

- *the wiping out of advantageous business rates for supermarkets*

- *measures to allow local authorities to find resources to fight planning applications by supermarkets*

- *stiff sanctions if supermarkets exceed the floorspace they are given planning permission for. Earlier this month, a Friends of the Earth report concluded that there is a growing trend for supermarket groups to flout restrictions.*

Supermarket chiefs insisted that they will fight off any plans to increase their business rates or tax their free car parks. And they urged regulatory authorities to resist calls for a time-consuming investigation.

Source: Nick Mathiason, The Observer, *29 January 2006*

Document B: Simon Hoggart's Week

It is heartening to see the wave of antipathy billowing out towards Tesco. And it is producing results too. Near where my parents live in Norwich, a persistent local campaign has stopped Tesco getting permission for a store that would wipe out a street of local shops, including two terrific butchers, a greengrocer, a fishmonger, an old-fashioned pharmacist who delivers, and two fine bakeries. Money spent with local people goes back into the community, to the plumbers, hairdressers, solicitors and dentists, whereas money given to Tesco winds up hundreds of miles away in Tescoland, wherever that is.

Source: Simon Hoggart, The Guardian, *25 February 2006*

> ### Document C: Total number of independent retailers, 2000–2004
>
> *2000 = 34,250*
>
> *2001 = 33,787*
>
> *2002 = 32,900*
>
> *2003 = 29,030*
>
> *2004 = 26,873*
>
> *Source:* IGD Convenience Retailing Report

Choices

The information and views contained in the documents suggest that it is likely that some kind of decision must be made about how to respond to the continued growth of the large supermarket chains. The following represent some options or choices that could be made:

- Allow supermarkets to carry on growing without any interference.
- Restrict the number of supermarkets a retailer can have in each region.
- Make it more difficult for the big retailers to get planning permission to build supermarkets.
- Ban outright the building of new supermarkets within a 10-mile radius of smaller towns.

Criteria

- The impact on local employment
- Environmental impact
- Consumer choice
- Public acceptability/opinion
- Cost

ACTIVITY 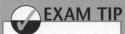 7

EXAM TIP

This type of question/task is likely to be worth a significant number of marks in the exam.

Select one of the choices given and evaluate it as a course of action through the application of some of the criteria provided.

Remember that you need to refer to the documents in a critical manner in order to support your evaluation.

See guidance on page 36

Some guidance

- You should spend quite a bit of time on this activity – it is important you practise tackling this kind of question.

- Before starting, read through Chapter 2 once more to remind yourself of the sort of points you should be making.

- Once you have finished the activity, make sure you study the more detailed guidance provided later in the book.

- Be sure to study carefully Chapter 5 *Preparing for the exam.*

SUMMARY

This chapter has helped you to:

- understand how evidence will help in framing a series of choices in response to a particular issue

- understand and explain how important it is to identify and apply relevant criteria in helping us to make decisions

- understand and explain some of the problems we might come across in applying criteria

- use criteria to evaluate choices in the context of evidence provided.

Identifying and defining dilemmas

Chapter 3 extends a process we started in Chapter 1 and developed in Chapter 2. Let's recap what we have done so far. We have:

- used evidence to explore some problems of definition
- used evidence to help us to identify and explain factors that might influence how people react to issues or problems
- identified appropriate choices in response to issues of concern
- identified and evaluated criteria which could be used in deciding upon courses of action
- used criteria to evaluate choices made.

In this chapter we will move on to:

- examine what we mean by the term **dilemma**
- identify and explain some dilemmas.

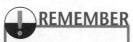

REMEMBER

Remember that a **dilemma** is a situation where a choice has to be made between two conflicting options, each of which will result in some undesirable consequences.

What is a dilemma?

You are likely to find the word dilemma being used frequently in situations where we are called upon to make decisions. Usually when people are using the word dilemma it is to describe some kind of difficult situation or problem.

For our purposes in Unit 3 we will define a dilemma as arising from a situation in which we need to:

- make a decision – we cannot simply avoid or ignore a dilemma
- choose between alternatives each of which will have some negative, or harmful, consequences. Bear in mind that the negative, or undesirable, effects of doing something may well arise from not doing something else
- deal with conflicting criteria. For example, the case of giving the morning-after pill to girls who are under age might meet the criterion of being easy to implement but may not meet the criterion of parental approval.

Expressing and explaining a dilemma

In the exam you will be required to identify and explain a dilemma that arises from the issue covered in the Resource Booklet. Therefore it is important that you learn how to express a dilemma clearly. If you do not express your dilemma clearly you will find it more difficult to suggest ways in which it might be resolved.

Before moving on to look at some real-life situations which throw up dilemmas, here are some useful tools that can help you when you are thinking about dilemmas:

- the harm test
- identifying where the interests of the individual conflict with the collective
- identifying conflicting criteria.

The harm test

One way of checking whether or not you have identified a dilemma is to apply what we might call the *harm test:* are the options you are putting forward in your dilemma each going to result in some kind of harm being done?

If the answer is 'yes', then you are likely to be on the right lines in terms of framing your dilemma.

For example, if you decide to detain indefinitely suspected terrorists, innocent people might be held against their will and deprived of their civil liberties. If you don't take this course of action, you may run the risk of releasing a terrorist leading to a serious attack and loss of life.

Identifying where the interests of the individual conflict with the collective

Many dilemmas revolve around the problem of trying to reconcile the interests of the individual with those of the various groups that we as individuals belong to.

We all, as individuals, have our own needs, demands, and expectations. But there are many occasions when these will conflict with the requirements of the **collective**.

KEY TERMS

Collective – the state or any organisation we might belong to, such as school, business, family and so on

For instance, we all value our freedoms or what we can call our civil rights, such as freedom of speech and the right to be tried by a jury. However, there are times when the government might think it necessary to deprive us of some of our civil rights in order to preserve public safety.

Identifying conflicting criteria

We have seen in Chapter 2 that when making choices we need to identify and apply criteria. However, the criteria we use to evaluate these choices might well produce conflicting results. Consider the following situation:

> *It is your duty as a school governor to decide whether or not to give permission for a school visit that involves outdoor activities such as rock-climbing and pot-holing. What do you decide?*

In order to help you make your decision, you would need to apply some criteria:

- One criterion we would have to apply here is that of risk.
- Another criterion could involve a consideration of personal development.

So in deciding whether or not to allow the visit to go ahead we need to strike some kind of a balance between conflicting criteria: let the visit go ahead on the basis that students will learn something about themselves and the importance of teamwork but accept the risk that they might get hurt; or stop the visit on the basis that we do not want to run the risk of accidents and therefore deny students a valuable experience.

In other words, what we have here is something of a dilemma:

> *Should the school governor give permission for outdoor activities that might involve health and safety risks or refuse permission and in the process limit possible personal development for the children?*

Identifying and explaining dilemmas: two case studies

Look at the following evidence about the medical drug Herceptin.

CASE STUDY 1

- *Herceptin targets the HER2 protein which can increase the growth of breast tumours.*
- *About a fifth of breast cancers are HER2 positive.*
- *Breast cancer is the commonest single cause of death for women aged 35–54.*
- *41,000 cases of the disease are diagnosed each year.*
- *At the moment (May 2006) Herceptin is only licensed for women with advanced disease, where it has spread in the breast or to another organ.*
- *It is estimated that 2000 British women suffering early breast cancer could die before Herceptin is available on the National Health Service.*
- *The cost of 1 year's treatment with Herceptin is £19,500.*
- *In 2006 an NHS Trust was taken to court by a patient because she had been denied Herceptin on the grounds of lack of evidence of its effectiveness. (NHS Trusts are responsible for running the National Health Service in each area.)*

The question we have to ask here is: what exactly is the dilemma facing the NHS Trust? This leads us on to our next activity.

ACTIVITY 8

Use the evidence on Herceptin to examine how far the choices facing an NHS trust represent a dilemma.

Use the following questions to explain your findings:

- What choice does the NHS Trust have to make?
- What negative consequences might result from whatever the Trust decides to do?
- What conflicting criteria might the Trust have to deal with?

 REMEMBER

Think about the three ways of expressing a dilemma to help you decide whether or not this is a dilemma.

Now look at the following report of a court case involving a vicar and his council tax.

CASE STUDY 2

A retired 71-year-old vicar yesterday became the first pensioner in England to be jailed for failing to pay his council tax on a point of principle.

He arrived at court carrying his toothbrush after refusing to comply with a court order that he repay the arrears on his council tax. He and his wife had paid an increase of 2.5% on their previous bill to cover inflation, leaving them only £63 in arrears, but with court and bailiff costs the amount now owed was £691.15. He was jailed for 28 days.

'We have been very patient with you', the magistrate told him. 'As you have failed to pay we have no alternative but to enforce the suspended prison sentence.'

The vicar replied by saying: 'The council tax has risen by 76% in the last few years. I am not paying it because it is an illegal tax.'

Afterwards the national anti-council tax pressure group Is It Fair? said: 'It is a really wicked tax, and upside-down world when a man goes to prison for withholding a portion of his council tax when you can hit someone over the head with a bottle and get a caution.'

The vicar's son said that his father was 'a man of principle and he might well go through all this again when he comes out. It all depends on how he finds the next 28 days.'

The vicar's wife said: 'The state of the council tax is a very serious issue. The Government needs to listen and put things on a basis of people's ability to pay.'

The Director of the Prison Reform Trust said: 'The average cost of keeping someone in jail for a month is more than £3000. Surely there must have been a cheaper way of dealing with the £63 originally owed?'

The Local Government Association said: 'We have consistently argued that council tax needs fundamental reform. This debate, however, cannot be used as an excuse for non-payment of council tax.'

Source: The Times, *8 September 2005*

In this case there are three main participants:

- the vicar
- the magistrate
- the local authority.

On one level or other, each of these participants in the case has decisions to make. It could be argued that in each case, whatever course of action is chosen, it will cause problems for those making the decision. In other words, each participant is faced with a dilemma. Let us examine the position of the vicar.

The vicar chooses to go to prison rather than to pay what he calls an 'illegal tax'. His son refers to him as being a 'man of principle'. Later on we will be examining the use of this word 'principle', but it is sufficient now to indicate that this issue of the council tax is more than just about the money as far as the vicar and his supporters are concerned. Either way, the vicar is faced with an awkward choice: 28 days behind bars with some potentially not very nice people; or pay up and risk losing the argument. Admittedly he is in a situation of his own making, and in a way he seems pleased enough to be going to prison in order to make his point and get plenty of good publicity. However, having got to this stage of being up before the magistrate, he now has a clear choice to make. He cannot decide both to go to prison and not to go to prison. Whatever he chooses to do, there will be some negative consequences. He is clearly faced with a dilemma.

ACTIVITY ❾

Examine the position of the magistrate and the local council in Case Study 2. Identify and explain a dilemma that they each face.

SUMMARY

This chapter has helped you to:

- explore what we mean when we talk in terms of facing a dilemma
- identify and explain a dilemma – how we frame a dilemma.

The resolution of dilemmas – applying principles

EXAM TIP

A major part of what you will be required to do in the exam is to develop and communicate an argument showing how you might resolve a dilemma. You should think in terms of spending something like half the time available to you in the exam on this task.

EXAM TIP
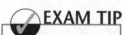

You will be required to use principles to help you resolve a dilemma. Whether you use practical or ethical principles will depend on the nature of the dilemma. Therefore, you do not need to memorise every one of the principles discussed in this book. However, the more knowledge and understanding you have of different types of principles, the more comfortable you should feel in applying them.

By this stage you should be feeling more confident when it comes to identifying and explaining dilemmas. Next you need to examine how we might attempt to resolve dilemmas – the single most important thing you will have to do in the Unit 3 exam. In this chapter we will:

- define and explain what we mean by principles
- examine some ethical theories and ethical principles
- explore how we might best apply some of these principles in attempting to resolve a dilemma.

Faced with the sort of difficult decisions we have been examining earlier, such as the Herceptin case on page 40, we might be tempted to feel that there is no solution. And you can argue that by its very nature a dilemma cannot, in truth, be satisfactorily resolved. (Think in terms here of conflicting criteria – see page 39.)

However, a dilemma, also by its very nature, is a situation wherein a choice needs to be made. In Unit 3 we need to demonstrate how we can attempt to resolve a dilemma through:

- identifying relevant principles (what we mean when we refer to 'principles' will be explained in some detail, but remember that we are looking at general rules that will apply to more than just an individual case and in a variety of contexts, for example *you should pay your taxes* is a principle).
- assessing the extent to which principles might be useful in helping us to make the sort of difficult decision posed by a dilemma.

And to enable us to take this process further we will also:

- examine how we might best use some ethical principles, or theories, in order to add clarity and weight to an argument based upon the application of principles.

Principles

What is a **principle**?

- A principle is not merely a rule. *You are not allowed to cycle on motorways* is a rule.

- A principle is a *general* rule which can be applied in a range of different contexts. *You must avoid acting so as to cause unnecessary harm to others* is a principle.

- Principles are often used in arguments as reasons.

- Arguments are often based upon principles in the form of assumptions i.e. they are the unstated reasons behind the claims that are made.

- A principle will often be used to form the basis of a recommendation. *A student caught stealing from the college library should be excluded from college* could be a recommendation based upon the principle that *stealing is wrong.*

Let's look back at the case of the vicar who would not pay his council tax and see how we can use this to illustrate the five points made about principles above.

- You must pay your council tax: this is the rule, or law, which the court is upholding when the magistrate tells the vicar that 'we have no alternative…'.

- The vicar's 'point of principle' can be expressed as a general rule: *you should not be forced to pay a tax which you consider to be a bad one.*

- The vicar uses his point of principle to justify not paying this particular 'illegal tax'.

- The vicar's wife is assuming that a tax *should* be based upon 'people's ability to pay'. (As we shall see later, this is one of the generally accepted principles of taxation.)

- The Local Government Association seems to be recommending that the law be upheld in this case based upon the principle that you should pay your taxes (even if you think they are unfair).

It is worth stating that we will be looking at two types of principle:

- practical (or pragmatic) principles
- ethical principles.

A practical (or pragmatic) principle relates to a specific practical aim and is often used for public policy-making.

An ethical principle considers what is morally good or bad, not simply what is practical.

We will concentrate on practical principles first and go on to consider ethical principles in some depth from page 50 onwards.

ACTIVITY ⑩

Read the following statement issued by the senior management of a sixth form college to its students. Relate the statement to the five points made about principles on page 44 by identifying:

i)   a rule

ii) a principle

iii) a principle used as a reason

iv) a principle in the form of an assumption

v)   a recommendation.

The College has decided that all vending machines will be removed from college premises as from a week tomorrow. Furthermore, no cans of fizzy drinks will be allowed on college premises as from next week.

The college does apologise to all students for any inconvenience that this might cause, but we feel that we have a responsibility to promote a healthy lifestyle for our students. This is in line with our anti-smoking policy.

The college would also like to take this opportunity to urge all our students not to use the local Burger Bar at lunchtimes. Choose one of the new healthy eating options available in our refectory instead.

Finally, we would ask all students to please refrain from dropping crisps and sweet wrappings anywhere on college premises.

Identifying relevant principles

As you might expect, certain principles are likely to be more useful in some cases than in others. A business, for instance, will base its operations on the principle that we should manage our time as effectively as possible. A television executive might operate on the principle that you should give the public what it wants and not what we think they should want.

It is important, when we come to resolving a dilemma, that we try to identify principles which are relevant to the problem we are discussing and which will help us to resolve it. These will be principles which we can readily apply to the situation we are dealing with and which will help us to come to a decision about the best course of action to take.

To illustrate what we mean, let us look at something we referred to in our comments on the case of the vicar and his council tax.

The principles of taxation

What makes a tax 'good'; and what makes it 'bad'? You might think that there is no such thing as a good tax, and tax exiles all over the world would probably agree with you. But, given that we live in a society in which the state provides protection and services on a collective basis, taxes are unavoidable in order to fund these. It would be difficult, for instance, to charge everybody separately for specific services like street lighting.

This is not to say, though, that we should not try to assess the relative merits of the different types of taxes we have, council tax included. We do have a way of doing this. According to Adam Smith, the founder of modern economic thought, there are four principles (sometimes known as canons) of taxation:

KEY TERMS

Equity – when we refer to equity in the context of what is the right or wrong way of doing things, we are talking about issues of fairness and impartiality

- **Economy:** a tax should not be too expensive to collect.
- **Certainty:** a tax should be predictable in terms of how much it will raise in revenue.
- **Ease of payment:** a tax should not be too difficult to pay or collect.
- **Equity:** a tax should be fair and reflect the ability to pay.

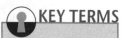
KEY TERMS

Ethical principles – are general rules or guides to action which can be applied in a range of contexts and are concerned with the notion of what is morally good or bad

The vicar's wife was appealing to the principle of **equity** because the tax should be based on the ability to pay, but had risen beyond inflation and the ability of people to pay. It is this principle which stands out from the other three. Can you see why this is the case?

The first three principles deal with what are largely practical, or pragmatic, considerations, while that of equity is connected more to values, to what we might consider to be morally good or bad. These are what we refer to as **ethical principles**, and we will be dealing with these in more detail later in this chapter.

When you come to apply principles to help make difficult choices you might decide that a practical approach is best, or at least that pragmatic considerations are important. Cost is one example that springs to mind. A particular tax might be seen as very fair but if it is also very expensive to collect then is it a good tax?

We can see, then, that economy (a tax should not be too expensive to collect) and certainty (a tax should be predictable in terms of how much revenue it will raise) represent the sort of principle that takes the form of:

> *If you want to achieve X then do Y.*

In this case, X represents the maximisation of revenue and Y represents a tax that will raise a predictable amount of money with minimum costs.

Applying the principles of taxation to a particular tax

It is very important in Unit 3 that you practise applying and evaluating relevant principles in terms of resolving the dilemma you are presented with.

When the government is faced with having to raise taxes, it could be faced with some hard choices. For instance, they may want to raise a large amount of money quickly and easily, but this might mean choosing to increase a tax that goes against the principle of equity – that a tax should be fair and reflect the ability to pay. Here, principles are being used as criteria to help decide upon the best option to take.

Council tax

- *Economy: A good tax will bring in a lot more than it costs to collect it.* Council tax is based upon where people live and a local authority has various ways to establish who lives where – electoral registers; benefits records; tax records, making it easy and therefore relatively inexpensive to collect.

- *Certainty: A good tax will yield in total what you have calculated.* A local authority knows the number of households there are in its area and what council tax band each property comes in. This ensures that you will receive in total more or less what you calculated.

- *Ease of payment: A good tax should not be too difficult to pay or collect.* For reasons given above, council tax is relatively easy to collect and people know how much they have to pay, when they have to pay by, and how they can make a payment.

Continued

- *Equity: A good tax will be one that reflects people's relative ability to pay;* *households with more money should therefore be paying more than the less well-* *off. While there are some exemptions from paying council tax (for example if you* *are on housing benefit) for those not exempt but on relatively low incomes, council* *tax is not fair. (Ask the vicar's wife.)*

Verdict

- *Council tax certainly has its merits as a tax when assessed against three of the four* *principles of taxation, but not on the fourth one. Whether you decide to increase it* *or not will depend on how much weight you place upon equity.*

- *The application of these principles should be of real use in helping the government* *to make decisions about taxation by enabling it to balance the advantages of a* *tax against its disadvantages and to predict the likely outcomes of a change in* *taxation.*

ACTIVITY 11

Apply the principles of taxation (concerning: economy, certainty, ease of payment and equity) to the tax on petrol. Use the same method as that used above for council tax.

Another application of principles

In the exam you will be dealing with an issue which the examiner will have selected from a wide range of possibilities. You will need to be skilled at selecting relevant principles to apply to whatever problem the evidence in the Resource Booklet will be concerned with.

With this in mind, let us examine another situation where principles play an important role: the courts and divorce.

The following extract concerns guidance given by the Law Lords to the lower courts on how they should decide on divorce settlements.

In their judgment, the Law Lords refer closely to what they see as being the relevant principles which should be applied in the difficult matter of deciding property settlements between a divorced couple.

How can the courts achieve fairness when dividing property after a divorce? As Lord Nicholls explained, in his leading judgment, that was the 'intractable' problem that the Law Lords were trying to solve in their ruling.

*Married couples committed themselves to sharing their lives: 'When their partnership ends, each is entitled to an equal share of the assets of the partnership – unless there is a good reason to the contrary. This **principle** is applicable as much to short marriages as to long marriages.'*

*Lady Hale, the only Law Lord to have specialised in family law reform, stressed the need for consistency and predictability in payments on divorce. She identified three **principles** that might guide courts in future cases: 'need, compensation and sharing'.*

She stressed, too, that conduct could not be taken into account by the courts unless it was both 'obvious and gross'. This approach, Lady Hale said, was not only just, it was the only practicable one.'

Source: The Daily Telegraph, *25 May 2006*

Judges in divorce settlement cases can be faced with having to make some difficult decisions. The situation they face does share at least some of the elements of a dilemma:

- The judge has to make a decision.
- Whatever is decided, there will be a negative reaction from one partner or other.
- We could view the competing claims of both partners as equating to conflicting criteria.

We can see, too, how judges formulate principles to help them to resolve such disputes. Phrased fully, the three principles identified here are:

> *Division of property should be determined by need.*

> *Division of property needs to take into account elements of compensation.*

> *Division of property should be determined by equal share.*

ACTIVITY 12

Use the principles identified by the Law Lords to help you to try to resolve the following case:

> Mr and Mrs Persimon were married for 4 years. When they got married, Mrs Persimon gave up her £70,000 a year job because they intended to start a family straight away. However, they were unable to have children.
>
> The marriage broke up after Mr Persimon confessed to seeing another woman. He has since remarried and has one child with his new wife.
>
> Mr Persimon had just started to set up a new business when he first met his ex-wife. This business is now worth £15 million. He has other assets of about £10 million.
>
> His ex-wife is now claiming she should receive a settlement worth at least £5 million. Mr Persimon is prepared to offer only £2 million.

✓ EXAM TIP

The intention is not for you to attempt to cram in as many principles covered in this chapter as you can. This would not represent good Critical Thinking. You will need to be selective. You will need to decide which principles are most relevant to the dilemma you are attempting to resolve.

Applying ethical principles to a dilemma: the principles of need, desert and right

Remember that in the Unit 3 exam you are required to identify principles to help you resolve a dilemma. You will obviously not know the issues you will be dealing with until you see the Resource Booklet in the exam. It will be very useful, therefore, if you have knowledge and understanding of the sort of principles you could apply to a range of cases.

One approach you can take is to look at principles based upon those referred to by one of the Law Lords in their divorce settlement judgment. We will now develop these in terms of looking at the concepts of **need, desert** and **right**. Principles based on these concepts could be particularly useful when dealing with problems of distribution.

Need

We could express this principle as:

> **We ought to distribute from each according to their ability to give to each according to their need.**

This means that all humans have equal worth but don't all start life on an equal footing. This imbalance should be rectified.

This principle can be used to establish that:

> *We should provide free care in the community for those elderly people who are less well-off.*

In the UK, the welfare state uses the tax system to establish funding to help those with particular needs.

How useful might such a principle be in helping us to make decisions?

- It could help us to allocate our resources in an objective and measurable way.
- It could be seen to be a humane and fair principle to adopt.
- It could help to prevent potentially damaging social divisions between the poor and the better-off.

What problems might we have in applying this principle in this case?

- It could prove to be very expensive to provide such free care as the number of elderly people is increasing.
- The elderly who would still have to pay for their care might complain that they were being penalised for working hard and saving up when they were younger.
- The government might then have to decide whether or not to provide free care for all.
- You could argue that this would be a better way to achieve equality of outcome – more people get free care and are therefore happier with the situation – but not equality in terms of the personal resources available to elderly people.

It is useful at this stage to consider the principle of desert.

Desert

We could express this as the principle that:

> **We ought to reward only those who merit (or deserve) it.**

This principle could be used to establish that:

> *Expensive medical care should be provided first to those who have worked hard and looked after their bodies the best.*

How useful might such a principle be in helping us to make decisions?

- It would be seen to reward, and therefore to encourage, people to work harder.
- It could lead people to take more responsibility for their own lives and to see the connections between what they do now and what happens to them later.
- It could encourage people to try to lead healthier lives, with benefits to society all round.
- It could turn out to be very cost-effective as people who look after themselves tend to need the NHS less than those who do not.

What problems might we have in applying this principle in this case?

- This could conflict with the principle of need.
- It would be difficult to assess who exactly are the most deserving.
- It would be seen to be discriminatory against groups such as smokers and drinkers.
- It could be argued that this principle supports inequality of opportunity, since some people cannot compete for the reward as well as others. This could be because of low incomes, lack of facilities, inadequate education, etc.
- It might widen the gaps in society, which could be seen as promoting injustice and resentment.

Right

KEY TERMS

Rights – moral or legal entitlements

Defining the term **rights** can raise the kind of problems of definition we looked at in Chapter 1 and can be the subject of much debate. We will use a broad definition of rights as moral or legal entitlements. Using the theories of egalitarianism and elitism can help us to subdivide theories of rights into two distinct approaches. Egalitarianism is the view that all humans are to be treated equally. Elitism is the view that some humans are entitled to privileged treatment in virtue of some genetic or social fact about them.

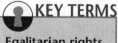

KEY TERMS

Egalitarian rights theory – humans have rights in virtue of their humanity, so we all have the same rights

An **egalitarian rights theory** would therefore claim that all humans have the same rights. We might express this as the principle:

> *There is a moral duty to provide for the basic human right to an equal share. Justice demands this.*

Elitist rights theory – people gain rights by virtue of social or genetic status so different people have different rights

In contrast an **elitist rights theory** would claim that people have different rights which they gain in virtue of their social or genetic status. We might express this as the principle:

> *There is a moral duty to respect certain social or genetic rights when deciding how to distribute resources.*

How might using a principle based upon an *egalitarian rights theory* be useful?

- It could be easy to apply as there can be a clear decision about how much each person gets.
- It can speed up decision-making and cut down on administration and fraud.

What problems might there be?

- It may lead to a lack of motivation as you will never merit any more than anyone else.
- It may conflict with principles based upon desert.

How might using a principle based upon an *elitist rights theory* be useful?

- It allows certain socially determined rights to be respected.
- It may help to preserve a sense of a stable, established order.

What problems might there be?

- It may cause unrest in society if these rights are disputed.
- It will conflict with principles based upon need.
- It may lead to social and economic stagnation.

ACTIVITY ⓭

Read the two proposals below and show how we could both justify and oppose them with reference to the principles of need, desert and right.

> *Child Benefit should be given at the same rate for everyone.*
>
> *Religious beliefs and values should be given precedence over secular beliefs and values.*

Using ethical principles to help us to resolve dilemmas

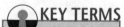
When the term 'principle' is used it is often used in the context of a **moral concept**. The study of what we consider to be morally good or bad actions is ethics. Remember that when we refer to ethical principles, we are talking about ideas and concepts to do with whether a course of action is considered morally good or bad.

Some important moral concepts

Moral concepts are ideas that help to determine how we think we should act, both as individuals and as a society. It is from these concepts that we will derive our ethical principles. Such concepts include:

- fairness
- rights
- good
- harm
- freedom.

Remember that our principles – our general rules – will be worked out in the context of these and similar ideas. Think back to the Law Lords trying to identify and explain principles that the courts could apply in order to achieve 'fairness'.

You cannot actually measure something like fairness. But you can attempt to work out some general rules, or principles, to help you to decide if an action is 'fair' or not.

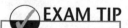
This is what you will be required to do when you are attempting to resolve a dilemma. The next section examines in some detail how we can approach this task – of resolving a dilemma – by using ethical principles. Remember that you will need to be selective about which of these principles are most relevant, or useful, to you in terms of resolving the actual dilemma you will be dealing with in the exam.

What is an ethical principle?

In attempting to resolve a dilemma we might very well adopt the approach that our best way forward is to examine the **ethics** of the situation. Here we would be concerned with ethical principles.

Ethics involves thinking and theorising about what is good and bad, what is the best way to live a good life. Whatever line of work you become involved in, you are likely to come across an ethical dimension to what you are doing. There are medical ethics, legal ethics and business ethics, to mention just a few. Ethics involves looking at how we make *moral* choices.

As we have already seen, some principles do not relate directly to moral issues. These principles relate to practical (or pragmatic) aims and are widely used to establish public policies. They can be thought of in terms of:

> *If you want to achieve this... then your principle should be...*

This makes it clear that the principle depends upon a particular aim. If you do not agree with the aim, then you can challenge the principle. Therefore, it would be important, if you wanted a particular policy or principle to be accepted, for you to convince others that the aim was acceptable.

An example of this might be:

> *If you want cleaner beaches, then it is right to raise local taxes.*

This principle relates to the practical aim of improving the cleanliness of the environment.

However, an ethical principle considers what is good or bad, not simply what is practical. Just as practical principles relate to practical aims which need to be accepted to avoid a challenge to the principle, ethical principles relate to a value which needs to be accepted to avoid a challenge to the principle. Therefore if you are going to recommend the use of an ethical principle, you will need to consider the acceptability of its underlying belief or value.

Consider the following opinion:

> *I believe that it is wrong to take a life. So, for me, abortion cannot be an option, unless a pregnancy endangers the life of the mother.*

It is clear that the general principle, *it is wrong to take a life,* has been used as a reason to justify decision-making in the specific case of abortion. This is clearly an ethical principle because it refers to the taking of a life as *wrong* (or morally bad).

Why do we use ethical principles?

An ethical principle is a decision-making tool which can help in a variety of both personal and public issues. It can provide a basic guide, which avoids working out each decision from scratch.

- **It saves time**: An ethical principle *if* true, should be true in all situations. Once accepted there can be no debate about whether or not it should be followed. Establishing a principle should therefore cut down the time taken in discussion about public issues.

- **Persuasion**: An ethical principle can also be an effective method of persuasion since if a recommendation is based upon a commonly held principle, such as *resources should be distributed equally,* then those who uphold the principle would need to agree to the recommendation or rethink their belief in the principle.

- **Rational response**: An ethical principle provides the opportunity for consistency in decision-making, as opposed to being guided by feelings which might be simply reactions to family, social or cultural influences.

Using ethical theories in the Unit 3 exam

- The exam is *not* meant to be seen as an ethics paper.

- You will not always have to use ethical principles in the exam. In some cases more practical, or pragmatic principles, might be as, if not more, appropriate in helping to resolve the dilemma. For instance: in making decisions about nuclear power we have to consider the practical principle that tells us that whatever form of energy we invest in it has to be one that we can afford.

- However, there will be few dilemmas that do not involve us in some kind of moral issue. For instance: in making decisions about nuclear power we need to consider the problem of nuclear waste that will be inherited by future generations. Do we have a moral duty to consider the well-being of people in the not-so-distant future? Do we have a moral duty to our planet as a whole?

- Although the specification for the unit does refer to various ethical theories, the intention is that you will select and apply principles that you feel are relevant to help you resolve the dilemma that you will have identified. These may therefore be ethical or practical principles.

What follows is meant as a broad guide as to how you can best use ethical principles in the exam. At the end of this chapter, however, we do outline some of the more specific ethical theories which you might find useful and interesting.

Making sense of ethical principles

The study of ethical principles involves examining various ethical theories which have been developed over centuries of human thought, and which are still being developed by modern philosophers.

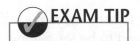
EXAM TIP

It will be important for you to distinguish between deontological and consequentialist principles in the exam.

You should think of ethical theories as dealing with over-arching principles. In other words, ethical theories attempt to develop a general principle from which we can work out whether any action is morally good or bad. For our purposes we are going to divide ethical principles into two main types:

- deontological
- consequentialist.

KEY TERMS

Deontological principles – rules of behaviour which are claimed to be right or wrong, regardless of the consequences

What are deontological ethical principles?

The word deontological derives from the Greek word *dentos* meaning duty. As an approach to actions this is the view that actions are morally good only if they are performed out of a sense of duty to uphold a principle, whatever this principle may be. A deontological approach to principles is the view that moral principles are to be accepted for reasons that have nothing to do with the consequences of accepting them, for example because they are intrinsically* correct or because they express the will of God. For instance some deontologists might argue that the principle *it is wrong to take a life* should be accepted because it expresses the will of God or because it is intrinsically right or both. However they would argue that this is the case regardless of any consequences that might result from the application of this principle, i.e. even if it meant the prolonged suffering of someone with a terminal illness.

__Intrinsically:__ in itself/inherently

How far are deontological principles useful in determining policies?

- **Brings clarity to decision making:** Such principles will be considered to be right regardless of the consequences. Therefore you do not have to consider exceptions or weigh up or predict the consequences of an action guided by such a principle.

- **Universal standards:** As everyone is expected to follow the principle, anyone breaking the principle should be relatively easy to identify.

- **Public knowledge:** This can be relatively easy to achieve, as the rules can be kept simple. Exceptions do not need to be set out, or defended.

- **They cannot be refuted:** If their overall justification is accepted for example if *'it is wrong to take a life'* is considered to be right because this is directed by God, then there can be little argument if those involved believe that God exists and that what God says is right. Similarly there might be agreement about the duty to protect the right to the freedom of speech if this is considered to be a basic human or social right.

What limitations might be met when applying deontological principles?

There are some significant limitations to this approach:

- **They do not take into consideration harmful consequences.** Deontological principles do not allow exceptions where the consequences are negative. Consider the situation of someone who is about to use a machine gun on an unarmed crowd, and the only way to stop this is by shooting at them from a distance. Would it be right to prevent a massacre by killing the person with the machine gun?

- **If two principles conflict there may be confusion over which should be followed.** Unless a hierarchy of principles is established – where if two conflict, the higher order principle should be followed.

- **Where there is a conflict of interest, there may be confusion.** For example, in the health service where funds are limited, it might be difficult to decide who should have the right to treatment.

Applying deontological principles to particular issues

Consider the following issue:

> *Should we reduce the number of weeks of pregnancy at which abortion is allowed?*

In June 2006, some Members of Parliament suggested that we should change the law on abortion by reducing the number of weeks of a pregnancy at which abortion would be allowed. How might the application of a deontological principle help us here?

- The number of weeks into a pregnancy might be viewed as irrelevant according to deontological principles. We might oppose the suggestion on the basis that there is a duty to do what is good and that doing good involves the preservation of life. Merely limiting the number of weeks when abortion is allowed does not, therefore, address the issue that all life should be preserved even if it is in the womb. This would not be very helpful to those who want to limit the number of abortions rather than banning abortion altogether.

- However, the issue could well revolve around a definition of 'independent life'. When do we classify a foetus as possessing life on the same terms as a baby? The answer to some people might be not until it is actually born. To others it might be defined in terms of how many weeks have passed since its conception. If we accepted the latter point of view then an application of deontological principles might still allow abortion under a certain number of weeks. It depends on how we define life.

ACTIVITY 14

Read the following passage about assisted suicide.

> *We are all likely to be faced with having to make some difficult decisions about death: either our own or that of someone close to us. If suffering from a terminal illness – or watching somebody for whom we care suffer – we might hope that a doctor would respect our wish that they withhold any treatment that would prolong life. We might even hope that a doctor might actually decide to treat the pain in such a way that it helps us to die more quickly. As the law stands, we will have very little choice. Should we change the law in some way so that people can be helped to end their lives in the case of terminal illness?*

What would be the result of applying deontological principles to this issue?

It can be seen then, that the application of deontological principles may be of some use to us when trying to resolve a dilemma, but that this use is limited. We shall move on to consider principles derived from a different moral theory – consequentialism.

What are consequentialist principles?

These principles justify a particular action by assessing the possible consequences of that action.

Consequentialist principles are thought to be more realistic than the deontological approach, as they recognise that a degree of harm is often the inevitable consequence of any decision. They believe that the best decision has to be the one that minimises this harm. This is thought to be achieved by weighing up the greatest good that could be achieved by the alternative decisions available.

What form can consequentialist principles take?

The basic formula for consequentialist principles could be expressed as follows:

> *It is right to choose those acts or rules that produce the greatest amount of happiness, or good, for the greatest number in the long run.*

This is the commonly accepted definition of Utilitarianism, which is the most frequently used consequentialist ethical theory. (See pages 65–66 for more information on Utilitarianism.)

Utilitarianism: the ultimate good is the greatest happiness for the greatest number

Consequentialist theories seek to decide which course of action or which rule is best, by measuring the amount of goodness produced. However, they might well differ as to what they consider to be good.

How far are consequentialist principles useful in making difficult decisions posed by dilemmas?

- **Realistic:** They recognise that in some situations a degree of harm is inevitable and they use reasoning to achieve the best possible outcome, sometimes as the lesser evil.

- **Practical:** They can offer a solution when there is a conflict of principles or conflict of interest.

- **Speed up the assessment of the consequences:** Past situations can be used as a guide in decision-making.

What problems might be met when applying consequentialist principles?

There are some significant limitations to this approach:

- Assessing the consequences to find out what is the right thing to do might make decision-making *complex, confusing and time consuming.*

- There may be disagreement as to whether *short-term* or *long-term consequences* should be assessed.

- It is often *difficult to predict the possible consequences* of a decision. For example, going to war might end atrocities quickly or lead to long, draw out reprisals from the country being invaded.

- It might be *difficult to weigh up the options* in that both quality and quantity are often involved.

Applying consequentialist principles to particular issues

Let's look again at the issue of reducing the number of weeks of pregnancy at which abortion is allowed. How might consequentialist principles help us here?

- What a consequentialist might say is that abortion should be permitted if the harmful consequences of not allowing abortion would outweigh the harm done to the foetus.

- Is reducing the number of weeks at which abortion is allowed likely to lead to more harm or less harm overall?

  ○ It might be possible to argue that the further the foetus develops, the more it may suffer as a consequence of the abortion. It could also be argued that the risks to the mother of abortion, in terms of physical and emotional well-being, might increase the longer the pregnancy continues. Both reasons may give us cause to consider reducing the number of weeks at which abortion would be allowed.

○ However, lowering the number of weeks of pregnancy at which abortion is allowed would reduce parental choice as well as significantly increasing the number of births. In which case, the sum total of harm to the community as a whole resulting from damaged or unwanted pregnancies is likely to increase.

ACTIVITY 15

Re-read the passage on assisted dying in Activity 14 on page 59.

What would be the result of applying consequentialist ethics to this issue?

Attempting to resolve a dilemma by applying both deontological and consequentialist ethics

The best approach to this task in the exam will be to apply both deontological and consequentialist ethics to the dilemma you will have identified. This is because the two different ethical approaches are likely to yield different, and probably opposing, answers. You should see these in terms of being your intermediate conclusions.

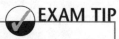

EXAM TIP

Remember that when you come to identify and explain a dilemma in the exam, you should be clear that you have identified a situation where whichever choice is made there will be some harmful, or negative, consequences.

This is what should happen in the case of a dilemma. It will then be your task to discuss the relative merits of each ethical approach in order to make some suggestions as to how, in the final analysis, we might resolve our dilemma. This should provide you with the main conclusion to your argument.

If you were to apply both ethical principles to our abortion dilemma, the dilemma could be expressed as:

> *Should we reduce the number of weeks of pregnancy at which abortion is allowed? Reducing the number of weeks of a pregnancy at which abortion is allowed may reduce parental choice and increase the harmful effects of damaged or unwanted pregnancies. However, not reducing the number of weeks at which abortion is allowed may preserve fewer lives (there may be more abortions) and may provide less protection against suffering for the unborn child.*

We have already examined the results of applying both deontological and consequentialist ethics to this situation but what conclusion can we come to? What is the resolution to our dilemma?

Applying the two principles appears to suggest two different resolutions:

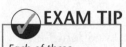
EXAM TIP

Each of these resolutions could be used as an intermediate conclusion.

1. The deontological approach states that there is a duty to do what is good. If we then go on to say that doing good involves the preservation of life, then we can argue that there is a duty to preserve life even if it is in the womb. This is true regardless of any harm that might result – from giving birth, for example, to a severely handicapped child.

2. The consequentialist approach would suggest otherwise. We must weigh the consequences – to the well-being of the unborn and to the well-being of both the mother and the baby if the pregnancy goes ahead, as well as the likely consequences to society as a whole.

We might consider that we have to accept choosing one ethical theory above another – in other words, that in a sense we cannot wholly resolve the dilemma because whatever we choose will be, in some way, both the right and the wrong thing to do.

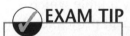
EXAM TIP

You should come to a conclusion based upon two or more principles which attempts to resolve the dilemma, even if the conclusion is a provisional one.

However, in this case, we could try to come to a resolution based on our definition of 'independent life'. If we were satisfied that up to a certain number of weeks a foetus is not classified as having 'life' in a generally accepted sense, then a deontological ethic as well as a consequentialist ethic, might allow that an abortion can go ahead. If we also held that there is a duty not to harm someone's health unnecessarily, then this would particularly be the case in situations where the health of the mother might suffer as a result of not having the abortion. If however, a foetus is considered to have 'life' from conception, then we might conclude that the dilemma cannot be resolved.

In the end we have to accept that whatever argument we put forward in attempting to resolve this dilemma will be open to counter-argument, sometimes fierce counter-argument. This arises from the very nature of a dilemma.

ACTIVITY 16

Use the results from the activities on assisted dying (Activities 14 and 15) to:

a) State and explain one dilemma that arises when making decisions about whether or not we should allow the terminally ill to choose when they should die.

b) Write an argument that attempts to resolve the dilemma you have identified by applying deontological and consequentialist principles. (You should comment in your argument upon the extent to which each of these principles might help you to resolve the dilemma.)

After reading this chapter so far and tackling the activities, you should feel that you are well-equipped to use principles to help you to resolve a dilemma. Further guidance on how you should go about this task is provided in Chapter 5. It is important for you to feel confident in this as it will be allocated a high proportion of the overall mark for the Unit 3 exam.

!REMEMBER

The principles you use to help you resolve a dilemma in the exam could be ethical principles, practical principles or a mixture of both.

The final section of this chapter provides you with more detail on various ethical principles provided by ethical theories (both deontological and consequentialist), which you should find interesting and useful. This section is followed by a table which provides a brief summary of some key deontological principles. You are not required to know all these theories and the principles they offer, but the more knowledge and understanding you have of ethical principles the more comfortable you should feel about applying some of them in the exam. Knowledge of a range of different principles should also provide you with greater scope for tackling whatever type of issue you are presented with in the exam paper.

Some ethical theories in more detail

Consequentialist theories

Utilitarianism

This is the most commonly used **consequentialist theory**.

Background

J Bentham developed the idea of maximising the happiness produced by actions. This was expressed as:

> *The ultimate good is the greatest happiness of the greatest number.*

Later in the nineteenth century J S Mill defined Utilitarianism as follows:

> *Actions are right in proportion as they tend to promote happiness, and wrong as they tend to produce the opposite of happiness.*

Underlying beliefs

- Human happiness or well-being is intrinsically good.
- It is morally good to maximise happiness/well-being.
- Consequences rather than motives are what should determine choice.
- Potential consequences can be measured. (Bentham constructed a complex **Hedonistic calculus** to enable this.)
- It is morally acceptable to break principles and rules, if by doing so a greater balance of happiness is achieved, because no specific moral principle is absolutely certain or necessary.

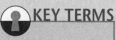

KEY TERMS

Hedonistic calculus – this involves using criteria to weigh up the happiness produced, for example, duration, intensity, scope, likelihood, people affected

Use

By assessing the consequences it is possible to make decisions where deontological principles give little guidance, i.e. where:

- rules conflict
- there is a conflict of interests
- the consequences of obeying a rule are negative.

Examples

- It is right to abort a baby when it endangers the mother's life.
- It is right to tell a lie if it prevents deaths.

Limitations

- It is sometimes difficult to judge which happiness is worth having as this involves questions about the purpose of life. Also some options differ in quality, for example:

> *In a natural disaster can you weigh up the cost of helping people as against the cost of saving places of international historic and artistic merit?*

- If happiness cannot be defined, people can use this principle to achieve their own ends/to promote their particular concerns.
- It is sometimes difficult to predict the consequences accurately.
- Weighing up the consequences (i.e. doing the calculations) can be complex.
- Motive is irrelevant; a good motive is not part of the calculus. Only the greatest happiness of those affected by the decision is counted.

Further varieties of consequentialist principles

The basic formula for consequentialist principles could be expressed as follows. You will see that that there are various ways of filling in the value to be gained, to whom it applies and the timescale involved.

> There is a moral duty to make those decisions that produce the greatest amount of ....(value) for ....(whom) in the ....(timescale).
>
> **Options:**
>
> | | | |
> |---|---|---|
> | happiness | the self | short-term |
> | pleasure | others | long-term |
> | love | everyone | |
> | justice | the greatest number | |

We have looked at one variation of the basic formula on page 66: utilitarianism (the greatest happiness for the greatest number). It may be useful to briefly consider some other consequentialist theories which differ in terms of what they accept from the list of options.

Differences in terms of the value to be achieved

Consequentialist theories seek to decide which course of action or which rule is best, by measuring the amount of goodness produced. However they differ in what they consider to be good. We have seen that happiness is considered to be the ultimate good in utilitarianism, another theory – hedonism, takes a slightly different approach.

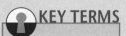

KEY TERMS

Hedonism – gaining pleasure and avoiding pain are what is required to achieve a good life

Hedonism

This theory considers that:

> *Gaining pleasure and avoiding pain are what is required to achieve a good life.*

There are various definitions of what pleasures humans seek, but in general, arguments tend to move away from immediate self gratification in physical pleasures, to the long-term virtues such as good reputation and tranquillity of mind.

Overall, in measuring the goodness of consequences, pleasure is usually seen in terms of those things that result in the greatest human well-being. This is expressed as the greatest amount of pleasure over pain.

Differences in terms of the consequences for whom

When constructing a principle to assess the consequences, it is important to decide whose best interest is being measured. Utilitarianism considers the best interest for the greatest number. Two further theories provide alternative views: egoism and altruism.

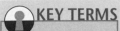

KEY TERMS

Egoism – a consequentialist theory which asserts that it is morally good to act in a way that would lead to the greatest good for the self

Egoism

This assesses: the greatest good for the self.

The term comes from the Greek *ego* meaning 'I'. The theory claims:

> *Decisions that maximise my well-being are morally good.*

This theory is often applied to those decisions that are seen to be matters of personal choice i.e. when the interests of others are not seen to be involved. For example:

> *This might be the basis of a decision taken by a landowner not to site a wind turbine on their land because of the noise and visual impact on their personal property.*

> *It might also be the basis for the decision of a busy parent who has decided not to recycle because the time taken to separate materials would prevent other tasks being completed.*

However, you would need to decide which other rights were being rejected in such decision-making, such as the rights of the environment. If this is considered to have rights, then egoism may not be always considered to be ethically appropriate.

KEY TERMS

Altruism – a consequentialist theory which asserts that it is morally good to act in a way that would lead to the greatest good for others, excluding the self

Altruism

This assesses: the greatest good for others, excluding the self.

This theory would support decisions that involve self-sacrifice. For example:

> *This might be the case where a property developer has the opportunity to build luxury apartments for executives which will reach the highest price. However, instead they choose to build low cost small apartments, to help local first time buyers, who would otherwise be forced to continue to rent.*

If there was no other motive, to make it easier to gain planning permission, it might be argued that the developer was being altruistic, as they would be sacrificing the larger possible profit.

Some would want to argue that altruism is never an option, as the alleged altruist might gain happiness from thinking of others and if they don't think of others, they might experience guilt. In this way decisions could never be considered to be totally altruistic.

Differences in terms of the timescale

When assessing the consequences of an action, it would need to be decided whether the effects to be judged are the *immediate* consequences or those in the *long-term*. One consequentialist theory which places importance on the long-term consequences is prudentialism.

Prudentialism

This assesses: | the long-term benefits, even if the short-term consequences are negative.

When faced with the decision of how to provide a third world community with clean drinking water, the decision to go for a long-term solution might be the prudential (wisest) option. For example:

> Investing in piping in drinking water might take longer to complete and cost more to install than providing bottled water. However if the installation and the cost of pipe maintenance were less than providing years of bottled water, this might be the greatest benefit for the community in the long run.

Deontological theories

Kantian ethics 1

Immanuel Kant believed that we can establish what our duties are by applying a principle he called the categorical imperative:

> Act only according to a rule that you can will to become a universal law.

Background

Kant's ethical theory is a frequently used deontological theory. He aimed to formulate a general principle underlying all moral choices (the categorical imperative above). His view was that moral rules can be worked out using reason alone and that moral rules should have universal application.

Underlying beliefs

- A moral rule can be worked out using reason alone.
- It becomes a moral rule if it can be willed without logical contradiction or inconsistency. (See examples below.)
- If a rule cannot be willed to be universal (i.e. that everyone follows this same rule), then it cannot be acceptable as a moral duty or be morally binding.

Kant's categorical imperative does not say that such and such an action is always wrong: rather it provides a general or overarching principle. It might be possible, for instance, to universalise both the rule that *you should tell the truth* and the rule that *you should do anything necessary to prevent innocents suffering.*

Use

This principle uses consistency and logic as its justification. Therefore it could be argued that it should have universal appeal, or at least a wide appeal to those who can, and who are prepared to, argue logically.

Examples

It can be used to establish:

> *You should tell the truth*

or

> *it would be inconsistent to will telling lies,*

as to universalise this would destroy the notion of truth.

> *It would be inconsistent to will stealing,*

as to universalise this would destroy the notion of property.

Limitations

- It is not sufficient by itself, as it cannot establish all moral duties. Some duties, such as to take care of the sick, poor and elderly cannot be established by logical inconsistency.

- If we interpret 'you can will' as meaning what we would be willing to allow, then it might be possible to morally justify things like inflicting pain, if we were willing to have pain inflicted upon us and have this universally applied. However it is likely that Kant meant 'act only according to a rule you can rationally and without inconsistency will to become a universal law'. Someone who didn't mind having pain inflicted upon them could then be considered as irrational.

- It relies upon people to accept the conclusions of logical reasoning, whereas a dictator might not always respond to reason.

- It does not resolve conflicts of duties, such as whether to prioritise economic or aesthetic responsibilities, as in a natural disaster where people and ancient art and buildings are all at risk.

Kantian ethics 2

> *Treat people as ends in themselves and not simply as a means to an end.*

Background

This is another part of Immanuel Kant's approaches to ethics.

Underlying beliefs

- Human beings have equal intrinsic worth.
- Individual human rights should not be violated.

Use

- It can be used to guard against:
  - some being exploited by others
  - some being sacrificed in the name of a cause.
- It is therefore useful in upholding equality and personal justice.

Examples

It can be used to establish that:

> *It is a duty to establish fair trade,*

Can the dropping of the bomb on Hiroshima be justified by the principles studied? Utilitarianism might justify it by saying that the deaths of a few potentially saved the lives of many. Kant's theory of ends would argue that it is wrong to treat those sacrificed only as a means to an end and not also as ends in themselves.

as without fair trade, those in the third world are being exploited. They are being paid lower wages than others elsewhere in the world who are performing similar tasks. This means that those people who are underpaid are being treated as a means to increase profits in other countries.

Limitations

- In upholding the equal intrinsic worth, the majority often lose out. For example, this principle would not allow the few to be sacrificed in war to save the many.
- It does not help in decisions concerning a conflict of human interests, such as between one nation and another, or between work and family, or family and friends. Whose interests would you choose?
- It cannot help with decisions about animals. It is difficult to use this with decisions about the environment unless it looks at not treating future generations as a means only.

Social ethics

Observe the social rights of others.

Background

A theory known as the social contract theory is based on the idea that a social agreement between individuals or individuals and the government is necessary to establish rights and that some liberty must be surrendered for the advantages of living in a well-ordered society.

The philosopher Locke argued that these moral or social rights and obligations pre-existed the creation of the state, so people could change the state if it failed to uphold these principles. In contrast Hobbes argued that the social contract *created* mutual obligations and social rights. This means the nature of these obligations could be defined by the social contract.

Rawls' theory of social justice defined these social rights as an entitlement which rational beings would agree upon, if they were drawing up the rules for an ideal society and they were ignorant of the position they would have within it. This is known as the veil of ignorance.

Underlying beliefs

- A social contract is necessary for us to live together in society. This should establish:
  - positive human rights, legal and moral
  - restrictions to enable the rights of others.
- These can be established by objective reasoning.
- There is a moral duty to observe these rights and restrictions when engaged in decision-making.

Use

It could be used to attempt to establish social rights.

Examples

It could be used to establish the moral duty to observe:

> *the right to a minimum wage*

since this might lead to a society with less poverty, if the rate was high enough. At the same time, it would have to be accepted that this would restrict the profits of employers.

> *the right to public non-smoking areas*

since this would protect the general public from passive smoking. Again this would be a restriction that smokers would need to accept, to uphold the right to a healthy environment.

Limitations

- It cannot establish universal rights if there are identified area differences, for example:

> *Social rights might differ according to national need, such as where freedom of speech is restricted to reduce unrest. Similarly, healthcare rights might be limited by lack of natural resources, for example, the right to clean water might be prevented.*

- It cannot help to resolve a clash of rights.
- It cannot help with decisions about animals or the environment.

Environmental ethics

> *Respect the natural balance of the world as a living organism.*

Respect the natural balance of the world as a living organism

Background

This is often referred to as the harmony of nature principle.

Underlying beliefs

- The earth is a great living organism in which everything is interlinked in a natural balance.
- This balance in its present or a previous state is good.
- There is a moral duty to maintain this balance.

Use

- This can be used to establish a non-anthropocentric approach to environmental decision-making, i.e. one that does not have the interests of humans at the centre of decision-making.
- It provides a long-term focus for decision-making, which allows the environment to be sustained for the future.

Examples

It can be used to establish that:

> *There is a duty to develop sustainable energy,*

since fossil fuels are being rapidly depleted. Sustainable energy through wind farms, solar energy and water power could also be argued to cause less pollution in the long-term.

It can also be used to establish that:

> *There is a duty to reduce carbon emissions,*

since not to do so is thought to contribute to global warming and by raising overall temperatures the balance of nature could change.

Limitations

- It may be an impossible principle, since with the natural extinction of species, the balance will change without man's interference.
- It may be an invalid principle since a 'dying' world, of which man is a natural agent, may be part of the overall balance of the universe.

Summary of some key deontological principles

Moral value behind the deontological principle *Belief in the value of:*	Over-arching principle *It is a moral duty to choose those acts or rules that:*	Justification *This duty is right because of belief in the value of:*	Examples of more specific principles that might follow from the over-arching principle
• divine rules	obey God's commands	divine authority	It is wrong to lie. It is wrong to steal.
• the universalisability of laws	you can logically will to become a universal law	logic, consistency	It is wrong to break a promise (because it destroys the notion of truth).
• humanity	treat people as ends in themselves and not just as a means to an end	value of the individual	There is a duty to establish fair trade. Capital punishment is wrong.
• rights determined by society	observe the social rights of others as set out by their community	society to determine rights	There is a duty to provide a minimum wage. There is a duty to provide public non-smoking areas.
environment • harmony of nature	respect the natural balance of the world as a living organism	the balance of nature	There is a duty to develop sustainable energy. There is a duty to reduce carbon emissions.

SUMMARY

This chapter has helped you to:

- understand the term 'principles'

- consider how principles and various ethical approaches might be used to help us to resolve a dilemma.

Preparing for the exam

In this chapter you will be given important guidance and strategies to help you tackle the Unit 3 examination.

There are five sections in this chapter, each of which you should pay careful attention to. They include:

- what the exam will assess
- what the exam will look like – the basic structure
- advice on how to answer each type of question
- an exam-style activity
- sample student answers with guidance from an examiner.

What the exam will assess

The examiner will be assessing your work on the basis of the three **Assessment Objectives** (AO1, AO2, and AO3) which are applied to all the Critical Thinking Units. These assessment objectives require you to:

- **AO1 Analyse** critically the use of different kinds of reasoning in a wide range of contexts.
- **AO2 Evaluate** critically the use of different kinds of reasoning in a wide range of contexts.
- **AO3 Develop and communicate** relevant and coherent arguments clearly and accurately in a concise and logical manner.

Important points to note

- The Unit 3 exam places more emphasis on how well you *develop and communicate your own arguments* than do the other papers. Over half the total marks for the Unit 3 exam will be allocated to this particular assessment objective (AO3). This will be reflected in the type of questions you are likely to be asked.
- The next most important assessment objective in the Unit 3 exam is AO2. *Evaluating different kinds of reasoning* will be allocated up to a third of the total marks.

- The quality of your *written communication* will also be assessed as part of AO3. For your work in the exam to be considered to be of a high standard in terms of written communication it should:
  - show that you can use a form of writing appropriate to complex subject matter
  - show that you can organise relevant information in a coherent manner
  - be legible and contain few errors in terms of spelling, grammar and punctuation. The meaning should be clear.

Using bullet points in the exam

While a bullet point-type presentation of your answers may well be fine, and should not prevent you from accessing the higher levels of marks, you should still be careful to set out your work in a way that makes sense and is relevant, coherent and easy to follow. This, after all, is the purpose of any presentation of good Critical Thinking.

What the exam will look like (the basic structure)

The Unit 3 exam will last for 1 hour and 15 minutes and you need to attempt all the questions.

The format will consist of a **Resource Booklet** and a **question paper**. You will answer the questions in the separate answer booklet provided.

The exact number and phrasing of the questions might vary from paper to paper, but in effect it is very likely that they will follow a pattern and process very similar to that explained in this book, i.e. you will be asked to:

- examine evidence, information and views presented in the Resource Booklet (approximately 20% of the total marks)
- comment upon choices and criteria relevant to issues raised by the evidence provided (approximately 30% of the total marks)
- frame and attempt to resolve a dilemma relevant to the topic under discussion (approximately 50% of the total marks).

The Resource Booklet

The Resource Booklet gives the topic or issue that will provide the context for you to demonstrate your Critical Thinking skills in a decision-making process. The topic itself could come from any one of a wide range of contemporary issues.

Make sure you take time at the beginning of the exam to study the Resource Booklet carefully. Read each document to get an idea of what it is about. The instructions on the front of the paper will advise you to spend 15 minutes doing this. This should be enough time, because it is important that you leave yourself a good hour to answer all of the questions.

The Resource Booklet will consist of four or five documents providing:

- information – explanations, instructions, guidelines; facts and figures, tables and graphs
- opinion – the views of experts, scientists, politicians, newspaper columnists, religious leaders, judges: people who we might refer to as 'opinion formers'.

The questions

Although the exam is not divided into sections as such, it is likely to follow this pattern:

- questions that will refer you directly to documents contained in the Resource Booklet
- a question that will require you to apply criteria in order to evaluate a particular course of action in the context of the evidence provided in the Resource Booklet
- a question or questions that will require you to frame a dilemma arising from the issues covered in the Resource Booklet and produce an argument which attempts to resolve the dilemma by applying relevant principles.

Advice on answering the questions
General points

- Remember to look at the number of marks given per question to help you work out how to use the time available in the most effective way. Some of the later questions in the exam will be worth a lot of the marks allocated overall.

! REMEMBER

Do not worry if you don't know much about the issue covered by the documents in the Resource Booklet. No specialist knowledge of the topic is required. It is how you *use* the evidence provided that will be assessed in the exam.

✓ EXAM TIP

Ensure that you manage your limited time effectively. It is vital you leave enough time for the final question – about 30 minutes.

- In questions which refer you to a particular document or documents, you should ensure that you are being seen to use the source referred to. This only needs to be done briefly – using a fact or figure from a source as evidence, or lifting a short phrase from it. You cannot hope for a really good mark if you fail to do this.

Using a particular document to identify and explain relevant factors (AO1, AO3)

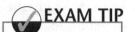

EXAM TIP

Remember to use some evidence from the document you have been referred to. This should add quality to your answer.

- Treat each factor separately – this is a good question to answer in bullet-point style.

- Note that the question asks you to *explain* as well as to identify. If you merely produce a list of relevant factors then the most you can expect is half the marks available for this question. (However, even if you are not sure how to explain the relevance of a factor, you will still gain a mark for listing it.)

- Try to think in terms of the different sorts of factors as outlined in Chapter 1: economic, political, social, health, and so on.

- Remember to select a relevant piece of evidence from the source you have been referred to.

Identifying and explaining problems of definition (AO2, AO3)

You should be thinking in terms of at least **two** problems of definition.

When you are considering possible problems of definition, think about factors such as:

- Context: who is using the words you are discussing? Where are they using them? Who is the likely audience? What is the nature of the topic or issue under discussion?

- Ambiguity: are terms being used in such a way as to be taken a number of ways? This can happen accidentally or be done quite deliberately.

- Specialist versus non-specialist use of language.

- The different ways in which different groups or societies might use key words and phrases, depending perhaps on different ethnic/political/religious/cultural perspectives.

- The use of certain words and phrases in such a way as to perhaps unduly/unfairly influence policy or public opinion to alter the terms of debate. (Here we might consider the impact of emotional and rhetorical language.)

Problems in using views as expressed in a particular type of source (AO1, AO2, AO3)

What you should aim for here is to identify and develop **two** relevant problems concisely, referring to the document in your answer. Depending on the document and the topic under consideration, relevant problems might include:

- On its own the source might provide a one-sided/unbalanced view; bias might be conscious or unconscious in nature.
- The authority of any views presented might be disputed or not clear.
- The views expressed might lack clarity.
- Such views might be contradictory.

Using the criteria to evaluate choices in the context of the evidence provided in the Resource Booklet (AO2, AO3)

The key section of the book here is Chapter 2, which guides you through the process of applying relevant criteria in order to help evaluate choices that could be made.

This type of question carries a substantial number of marks. So you should be looking to spend as much, if not more, time on this question as on the three previous questions put together.

When answering this type of question, bear in mind the following points:

- Make it clear from the start which choice you are going to evaluate.
- It will not be necessary for you to use all the criteria provided, but it is likely that a good response to this question will require that you use more than one criterion.
- Select a choice that is likely to let you apply a number of the criteria in a solid and sustained manner.
- Look again at the documents before selecting from the choices – there could be more evidence relevant to some of the choices than to others.
- Ensure that you do refer to the documents, and in a selective and critical manner.

- Be sure to come to a *conclusion*. Check that you have stated clearly what the end result of your evaluation is. Is the choice under discussion likely to be viable/effective/acceptable, etc. in the light of the evidence provided in the Resource Booklet? Remember that you will need to base your conclusions on a careful, though concise, consideration of a number of the criteria, while referring to the documents. You should also include as part of your evaluation some *intermediate conclusions*.

Attempting to resolve a dilemma (AO2, mainly AO3)

This question will carry the most marks. A close re-reading of Chapter 4 is the key to doing well in this question.

Most of the marks for this question are given for AO3. In other words, on the basis of how well you develop and communicate your argument.

In this part of the exam you will have to respond to a question or a number of sub-questions that will require you to:

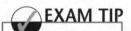

EXAM TIP

Take time to frame your dilemma – this will help you a great deal when you go on to apply principles to it.

- identify and explain a dilemma, which arises from the context of making decisions related to the issue covered in the Resource Booklet. You will need to frame your dilemma carefully (see Chapter 3) as it forms the basis of the final question on the paper. Remember a dilemma occurs where you have a decision to make which will result in some negative consequences either way (which will be reflected in conflicting criteria).

- present an argument in which you apply some *relevant principles* to your dilemma. You will need to consider more than one principle, though a very good treatment of **two** clearly defined and appropriate principles can access the higher marks. The principles you apply might be ethical or practical or both. What's important is that they are relevant to the dilemma you have identified.

Using principles

- You should avoid using ethical theories in a formulaic manner. For example, it would not be enough to merely state the utilitarian point of view; you also need to demonstrate how this might help you to resolve your dilemma in order to gain a good mark.

- Apply sufficiently different principles. For instance, you could apply a principle which judges an action on the basis of its *consequences* and a principle which puts more stress on our *duty* to do what we consider morally right regardless of the consequences.

- Assess the extent to which the principles you are using are helpful in trying to resolve the dilemma you have identified.

- Check that the reasoning you are presenting is logical and not flawed or based upon too many questionable assumptions. Your use of evidence and examples should be strong and valid.

- Ensure that you reach a conclusion in which you show how you might at least attempt to resolve the dilemma. This conclusion might well be based upon intermediate conclusions arising from the application of different principles to the dilemma.

An exam-style activity

 EXAM TIP

Remember how vitally important it is to read each question on the exam paper very carefully. Given the time pressure you are under it is very easy to overlook subtle differences in the wording of questions which vary from paper to paper.

ACTIVITY 17

Allow yourself 1 hour and 15 minutes to tackle this activity. Then compare your answers with the sample answers given on pages 88–98. This activity is not meant to be exactly the same as an OCR paper, but offers questions based on the assessment objectives.

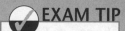 **EXAM TIP**

Spend 15 minutes studying the Resource Booklet before answering the questions.

There are three parts to this activity:

- resources
- lists of choices and criteria
- questions.

You should study the documents carefully. Allow sufficient time to do this. (In the exam there are likely to be four or five documents and you are advised to spend 15 minutes reading them.)

Resources

Document 1

Some statistics related to alcohol use in Britain:

- 90% of British adults drink alcohol.
- Britons spend £30 billion on alcohol each year.
- Alcohol costs employers £6.4 billion a year in lost productivity at work.
- The National Health Service spends £1.7 billion annually treating alcohol-related illnesses.
- Alcohol-related crime costs £7.3 billion every year.
- Another £4.7 billion is spent every year on the human and emotional cost of alcohol-related crime.
- Some 22,000 people die prematurely each year as a result of alcohol misuse.
- Each year the government raises £7 billion through taxes on alcohol.

Source: www.newsvote.bbc.co.uk, 15 February 2006

Document 2

Some views on alcohol abuse:

The government: *Ministers are planning to publish a strategy to tackle binge-drinking and other alcohol-related problems. Home Office Minister, Hazel Blears, said changes to pub opening hours would also help. She said that the licensing bill [implemented in December 2005] would help tackle the problem by removing a single closing time and reducing disorder in town centres.*

Ms Blears told Radio 4's Today programme:

'Young people will say to you, "We have a lot of education about drugs, but not enough information about alcohol". Information means they can make choices, so I think education and prevention is going to be a big part of our policy.'

The pub trade: *'Alcohol misuse needs tackling and treating. We also need to get to the root causes of what motivates a significant number of people who think it is acceptable to go out on a Friday and Saturday night, drink to excess and indulge in anti-social behaviour.'*

Rob Hayward, Chief Executive of the British Beer and Pub Association

Alcohol-related charities: *'We are talking about families dissolving in a sea of alcohol.'*

The Chief Executive of Turning Point

'More money should be invested in alcohol services, as they are seriously under-funded at the moment.'

Alcohol Concern

A political opponent of the government: *'The government has been far too complacent about the problem of alcohol abuse – particularly among young people.'*

Oliver Letwin, the Shadow Home Secretary

Source: www.newsvote.bbc.co.uk, 15 February 2006

Document 3

What the newspapers said about the new Licensing Laws introduced in 2005:

Tony Blair can hardly claim he was not aware of the binge-drinking problems relaxation of the licensing laws would bring. Police, judges, MPs and local councils queued up to say all-day drinking would lead to an explosion of the booze-fuelled violence we see in our towns and cities.

The idea that relaxing the laws would turn us into a Mediterranean culture where we drink one glass of wine over a meal was laughable... Britain's drink-crazed youngsters' ambition on the weekends and on their holidays is to drink as much as possible as quickly as possible. This is the British disease.

Source: Daily Mirror, *11 August 2005*

Criticisms of the new law are fallacious. The number of pubs that have applied for a 24-hour licence has not even reached double figures, and while 90% of the 47,000 pubs in England and Wales have applied for an extension of their drinking hours, the vast majority have merely asked for an extra hour or two on Fridays, weekends and public holidays.

This is not to excuse the unacceptable, violent and anti-social behaviour that is inextricably linked with binge drinking, particularly among young men. But the current, rigid laws [those in place before November 2005] are fuelling these problems, not resolving them.

Source: Maxine Frith, The Independent, *11 August 2005*

Exam question

Choices and criteria

Choices

In any situation where we have to make decisions we are faced with a number of choices. In the case of responding to problems connected to alcohol abuse, the following represents a series of choices that could be made:

- Persevere with the new licensing law as introduced in 2005.
- Bring about a large increase in government spending on educating and informing people about the dangers of alcohol abuse.
- Scrap the new licensing law and introduce more restrictions on opening hours for pubs.
- Introduce much more severe punishments for those caught serving alcohol to under-age drinkers.
- Stop supermarkets from selling alcohol.
- Bring in heavier taxes on drink to make it a lot more expensive.
- Make patients with alcohol-related illnesses pay for their own treatment if they will not promise to give up drinking.

Criteria

In dealing with the issues raised by drinking we need to develop criteria that can be used to help us to make choices. Examples of such criteria might include the following:

- cost
- risk
- effective use of resources
- public acceptability
- enforceability
- legality
- equity.*

*Equity: the quality of being fair and impartial.

Questions

Attempt all the questions (be sure to note the number of marks given for each question).

1. Refer to **Document 1**. Identify and explain **three** factors that might affect how people view the issue of drinking in Britain.

   (6 marks)

2. Refer to **Documents 2** and **3**. Explain why the term 'binge-drinking' might present us with problems of definition.

   (4 marks)

3. Refer to **Document 3**. Explain some of the problems in using the views of the two newspapers in assessing the likely effects of the new Licensing Law introduced in 2005.

   (6 marks)

4. Select **one** of the choices provided in the list on page 86 and evaluate it as a possible course of action. In your evaluation you should:

   - use some of the criteria provided
   - refer to the documents in the Resource Booklet.

   (24 marks)

5. Present an argument that attempts to resolve a dilemma that might arise when making decisions about dealing with the alcohol problem in Britain. In your argument, you should:

   - state and explain a dilemma arising when deciding how best to respond to the issues raised by drinking in Britain
   - identify some relevant principles
   - discuss how helpful these principles might be in helping to resolve the dilemma you have identified.

   (40 marks)

   Total marks = 80

Sample answers for Activity 17 and commentary

The sample answers that follow represent the type of responses that would gain high marks in the Unit 3 exam. For the sample answers to questions 1–3 we have underlined where the response deserves to be credited. Details of how and why each answer deserves to be credited are given in the margin close to the relevant text. Each answer then ends with an examiner's comment.

Question 1

*Refer to **Document 1**. Identify and explain **three** relevant factors that might affect how people view the issue of drinking in Britain.* **(6 marks)**

What you are required to do here (three times) is to identify a relevant factor and then to develop your answer in order to explain its relevance.

Factor identified; some development supported by evidence from Document 1 = 2 marks.

Factor identified; some development supported by evidence from Document 1 = 2 marks.

Factor identified; some development supported by evidence from Document 1 = 2 marks.

Sample answer

<u>Crime and fear of crime</u> are factors that play a large role in a lot of people's lives. <u>Older people, in particular, are likely to be very influenced and concerned</u> when they see that drink-related crimes cost this country <u>£7.3 billion a year.</u>

The effects of drinking on the <u>economy is also a factor</u> to be taken into account when looking at how people might react to the issue of drinking in Britain. <u>Employers are going to be concerned at the £6.4 billion (Document 1) cost to their businesses due to the effects of drink on their workforce.</u>

There is also a <u>political factor</u> to be taken into account here. Document 1 tells us that <u>£7 billion is raised every year from taxes on alcohol. The <u>government's view of the drink problem could be affected here because if people start to drink a lot less then other taxes might have to go up and the public might not like this.</u>

Examiner's comment: The candidate has answered this question concisely and precisely; each factor is relevant and developed/supported by clear and appropriate reference to the document. Total = 6 marks.

Question 2

*Refer to **Documents 2** and **3**. Explain why the term 'binge-drinking' might present us with problems of definition.* **(4 marks)**

To get all four marks the best approach here will be to identify and to explain clearly two problems of definition arising from the term 'binge-drinking'.

> **Presents a problem of definition; develops/explains the point; refers to document = 2 marks.**

> **Suggests a possible problem; refers to documents; develops/explains point = 2 marks.**

Sample answer

A problem of definition presented by the term 'binge-drinking' is that it might well be defined by a <u>medical professional in a particular and precise way and by others in a different, broader sense</u>: a doctor might refer to binge-drinking as an <u>exact number of units of alcohol consumed</u>. <u>While we</u> might infer from <u>The Daily Mirror's editorial (Document 3)</u> that 'binge-drinking' is to be equated simply to <u>'all-day' drinking</u>.

Another problem of definition could be related to how <u>different groups perceive binge-drinking.</u> The politicians and newspapers in <u>Documents 2 and 3</u> would <u>define binge-drinking as a wholly harmful activity to be discouraged.</u> Whereas the 'young men' referred to by <u>The Independent</u> might <u>define binge-drinking as an enjoyable activity that helps them to relieve the stresses of a busy working week.</u>

Examiner's comment: The candidate's has made a valid attempt to present two different problems related to definition, in which the documents have been used to develop each point. Total = 4 marks.

Question 3

*Refer to **Document 3**. Explain some of the problems in using the views of the two newspapers in assessing the likely effects of the new Licensing Law introduced in 2005.* **(6 marks)**

Try to identify and explain at least *two* problems. A very good treatment of two problems should get you 6 marks. Remember that you must include some reference to Document 3.

A problem is clearly identified and developed. Candidate clearly explains why bias could be a problem with reference to the document = 3 marks.

Problem clearly identified and developed with reference to document. Candidate shows clearly that the contradictory views expressed might make it difficult for us to know who to believe = 3 marks.

Sample answer

One problem could be that of <u>political bias</u>. In other words, a deliberate distortion of the evidence and presentation of a picture to suit the newspaper's own views and affiliations. <u>If such bias is present then we will need to use the views of the newspapers with considerable care when it comes to assessing the effects of the new law. The Mirror, for instance, does seem to want to criticise the Prime Minister – 'he can hardly claim he was not aware'.</u> Although the paper might be genuinely concerned about 'booze-fuelled violence' and alcohol abuse, <u>it may be guilty of exaggeration in order to appear to make the case against the new law stronger. We do not know if The Mirror may have simply ignored evidence contrary to its views. The Independent seems to be implying just this when it claims that 'criticisms of the new law are fallacious'. However, The Independent itself might support the current government and thus want to present a more favourable picture of its policies.</u>

Another problem could be that the two newspapers used in Document 3 <u>tend to contradict each other.</u> <u>The Mirror</u> suggests that the new law has resulted in <u>large-scale changes in drinking hours</u> and that the <u>result will be disastrous</u> - an 'explosion' of drink related incidents. While <u>The Independent implies that the new law was needed</u>, to replace the 'current, rigid laws'; that, in fact, it was the old laws that were part of the problem. <u>So the problem could be, who do we believe? We might decide that The Independent is being more reasonable because it does provide some evidence to support its views, i.e. the very small number of pubs applying for 24-hour licenses. But The Mirror might be a truer reflection of public/expert opinion.</u>

Examiner's comment: The candidate demonstrates a clear understanding of the question and presents two problems which are explained and developed with clear reference to the sources. Total = 6 marks.

Question 4

*Select **one** of the choices provided in the list above and evaluate it as a possible course of action. In your evaluation you should:*

- *use some of the criteria provided*
- *refer to the documents in the Resource Booklet.*   **(24 marks)**

Remember that to answer this question well you should:

- use the criteria to judge whether or not the choice you are looking at is likely to be a good one. Remember that this is what the criteria are there for – to help us make decisions from a number of choices open to us
- start by stating clearly which of the choices you will be evaluating
- state which criteria you will be applying
- use the documents.

Notes on response levels

- This question will be marked in terms of which level of response the examiner thinks your answer belongs to.
- There are four levels of response. A Level 4 (L4) response will be one that deserves to be credited with a mark between 19 and 24.
- The sample answer below is one that we think is worth a L4 mark. This means that it exhibits *some or all* of the following qualities:
  - a sound and perceptive selection of appropriate criteria to one of the choices, with clear indications throughout of a firm understanding of how the application of different criteria might well be used to strengthen/weaken the case for choosing a particular course of action
  - confident and critical use of the resource material
  - coherent and convincing reasoning that is well-structured
  - a good standard of written communication, with a few only minor inaccuracies, if any.
- We have indicated where and how we think the candidate has exhibited L4.

A good start, appropriate criteria clearly identified; possible early indication of a L4 response.

Good appropriate critical use of evidence – more of this will indicate a possible L4.

Some clear indications of a L4 response here: candidate has shown clearly how applying this criterion might well both strengthen and weaken the case for choosing this course of action; Document 1 has been used with some indication of its limitations.

Sample answer

Choice: Bring in heavier taxes on drink.

The criteria that seem to be the most relevant in evaluating this choice as a course of action are: cost; effective use of resources; risk; and public acceptability.

The evidence provided in Document 1 sets out to illustrate just how much British drinking habits are costing the economy, the government and society as a whole. While we might want to question the meaning and significance of some of the figures supplied here – such as, what exactly is being referred to by 'the human and emotional cost' of alcohol-related crime? – it would seem to be clear that the criterion of cost is going to be very relevant when it comes to evaluating any policies to tackle the drink problem in this country.

Raising taxes on alcohol would appear to have the benefit of carrying few, if any, extra costs to the government as it is a course of action that does not involve setting up an extra government department or anything like that to implement it.

However, it could also be argued that bringing in heavier taxes on alcohol could have negative effects in terms of cost. Document 1 tells us that £7 billion a year is raised through taxes on alcohol. Any substantial loss of this revenue, due to a fall in the sales of alcohol, could actually reduce the total amount raised by taxes on drink and this could result in the government having to raise other taxes, which might raise costs elsewhere. (However, the figures in Document 1 do not enable us make such calculations.)

Applying the criterion of cost to the choice of bringing in heavier taxes on alcohol could, therefore, produce some mixed results.

A confident and critical use of the source material; L4.

Critical use of source, not taking views at face value.

Shows a clear understanding of how a criterion can be used to argue both for and against a course of action; L4.

The criterion of cost is, of course, closely linked to that of the effective use of resources. The resource material would suggest that the choice of bringing in heavier taxes on drink might well represent an effective use of resources. It could be argued that such an increase in taxes would provide us with the money needed to invest in alcohol services. Alcohol Concern in Document 2 indicates that not enough resources are being put into alcohol services, while the Home Office Minister claims that education and prevention should play a large part in policies on alcohol abuse. The minister's views might be influenced by a motive to defend the new licensing laws, while Alcohol Concern as a pressure group might be considered to have a vested interest to argue for more resources as a matter of course. However, both the minister and the pressure group are likely to be very well-informed about the drink problem and so their views should carry a lot of weight.

However, once we come to apply the criterion of risk, we get a more mixed assessment of raising taxes as a course of action. The Mirror's account of a 'drink-crazed' culture might be seen as a colourful exaggeration aimed at pleasing its older readers; while its view of young people obviously represents a gross generalisation, not to say a slippery-slope. But it is to some extent born out by other sources. The Independent, which evidently supports the new licensing laws, still refers to 'unacceptable... antisocial behaviour' amongst young men. Merely increasing the price of drink might well not be enough to deter such people from getting drunk and the risk might be that they will get hold of the extra money by any means possible, including theft, etc. However, we need to balance this risk against the opposing risks to health of not attempting to make people cut their drinking by making it more expensive.

Continued

Finally, we must consider with any measure such as a large increase in taxes how the public might react. Any government, for instance, is very likely to use a criterion of public acceptability in evaluating a possible course of action. This is not just a matter of losing or gaining popularity, but a recognition that the most effective policies are likely to be those that are, at least in principle, most acceptable to the public at large. The very large costs illustrated in Document 1, if widely enough known, might well indicate that there could be quite a lot of support for increasing taxes on drink. However, it would seem that the government believes that education is a better answer (Document 1). But this might be because the Home Office Minister does not want to suggest a step that will hit people in the pocket which might run the risk of a loss of support.

The criteria used here to evaluate bringing in heavier taxes on drink have produced some mixed results: it may turn out to be cost-effective and perhaps gain public approval, but it is also a course of action which might prove risky and have negative effects on overall government revenue.

> **A useful application of a criterion to the choice in the context of the evidence.**

> **Presents a balanced case in terms of evaluation.**

Examiner's comment: The candidate has applied a more than sufficient number of relevant criteria very effectively to produce a balanced assessment of one of the choices. The reasoning has been convincing and resource material has been used with some discrimination. Standard of written communication is very good. Level 4.

Question 5

Present an argument that attempts to resolve a dilemma that might arise when making decisions about dealing with the alcohol problem in Britain. In your argument, you should:

- *state and explain a dilemma arising when deciding how best to respond to the issues raised by drinking in Britain*
- *identify some relevant principles*
- *discuss how useful these principles might be in helping to resolve the dilemma you have identified.* **(40 marks)**

Remember that to answer this question well you must:

- identify a situation in which we can see a possible dilemma
- explain why it is a dilemma (there are some negative consequences whichever way you decide/conflicting criteria)
- clearly identify some (at least **two**) principles relevant to the dilemma
- assess the extent to which these principles are helpful in resolving the dilemma
- reach a conclusion that represents an attempt to resolve the dilemma (in which you might recognise that any such attempt is unlikely to be wholly successful).

Again, what we have below is a response which we think is worth a L4 mark. A L4 answer is one that will be credited with between 31 and 40 marks.

A dilemma has been clearly identified and explained in terms of negative consequences and conflicting criteria are clearly implied; high L4.

Sample answer

The dilemma: should we deny patients expensive treatment for alcohol-related illnesses if they refuse to give up drinking? If we decided to deny treatment in such circumstances then this is likely to result in suffering and perhaps death for some patients as well as being seen to deny people an equal right to treatment. But if we do not deny treatment in such cases then this might mean using scarce medical resources in cases where a patient is unlikely to benefit from such treatment instead of treating more patients who will gain real benefit.

Relevant principles that we can apply to this dilemma are ones that derive from consideration of Needs, Deserts and Rights. Such principles could be expressed like this:

- We ought to provide health care, first and foremost, on the basis of need.

- We ought to first reward or care for those in society who merit it the most.

- We have a moral duty to provide for the basic human right to enjoy an equal share in the benefits of our society.

Relevant principles clearly identified.

Continued

A well presented application of the principle so far; indicating L4 so far.

In applying the first principle to our dilemma, it would appear to be clear that, in accordance with such a principle of need, we should not deny treatment to any sick person on the basis that they have brought their illness on themselves. After all, acting on the basis of this principle, we do not deny treatment for injuries which are self-inflicted, as a result, for instance, of playing rugby or going rock-climbing. We can also argue that if we did decide on a policy of denying treatment to those who will not promise to give up drinking then this would place doctors in a difficult situation; they might have to deal with the anger of patients and their families, as well as being accused of 'playing God' with people's lives.

However, applying a principle based upon need does have its limitations in this case in so far as helping us to resolve our dilemma. It does not, for instance, help us to decide which of two equally ill patients should get a liver transplant first. In such a situation a doctor might have to apply a more pragmatic, or prudential principle based on which option would be the most likely to bring about a successful result. Giving a new liver to a heavy drinker with a bad liver but who is unlikely to give up drinking could be seen as being a waste of a valuable resource. The utilitarian principle of the greater good could also be used here. What would be more likely to lead to the greater good? Providing medical treatment where and when it was most likely to be effective seems to be a sensible and right answer. But having a general rule that allows doctors to decide on who gets treatment on the basis of lifestyles might result in more harm than good.

A sustained discussion of the uses and limitations of principles; L4.

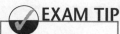

Again, the candidate is discussing what might be the conflicting results of applying different principles; refers to principles based upon deontological concepts; L4.

Another good exposition of a relevant principle; L4.

What happens if we decide to apply a principle based upon the idea that people should get their 'just deserts' – what they deserve? We could argue that this would have the benefit of encouraging people to look after themselves better and of rewarding those who live healthier lives, thus adding to the greater good by being more productive at work. (Document 1 shows how much drinking costs the economy in lost productivity.) You could also argue that we have a duty to look after our bodies and health in order to make the most of our God-given talents. This could be viewed as a deontological principle, based upon doing what is right rather than just looking at the consequences. Although the effects of healthier living are likely to be beneficial, what about activities that involve high risk while developing our talents, such as extreme sports? In terms of our dilemma, we can see that a principle based upon deserts might be of help but also pose some difficulties. A drinker might claim, for instance, that they have paid more taxes than a lot of other people as well as helping to keep brewers and bar staff in work, and so deserves treatment as much as anybody else.

The main problem with deciding who should receive what treatment on the basis of who is most deserving is that it would be seen as being discriminatory and as widening the divisions in society. This brings us on to the principle based upon a concept of the basic human right to enjoy an equal share of the benefits provided by our society, in this case access to medical treatment. This would fit in with the egalitarian values of a democratic society and could be seen as preventing discrimination on grounds other than of need and objective medical opinion. Also, it could be argued that a fundamental right has to be respected regardless of the consequences – a deontological ethical viewpoint.

Continued

Reaches a conclusion which recognises the inherent difficulty of resolving a dilemma; L4.

However, we still come up against the problem – and thus the dilemma – of what to do in cases where we have to choose between competing rights and where applying different principles might appear to lead us to different conclusions. If we do deny treatment to the unreformed heavy drinker then we will be accused of denying them a basic right as a citizen as well as introducing a possibly harmful discriminatory principle into the health service. On the other hand, not denying treatment could be seen as a waste of resources and result in the denial, or delaying, of urgent treatment to a more deserving patient who would probably benefit more from the treatment in the long run, with associated benefits to society as a whole. Because of the very nature of a dilemma, such a decision will always be a hard one. In this case we might decide that as long as the patient has been given a clear and informed choice of giving up drinking or not then it is their right and duty to exercise that choice. In which case, we might be justified in denying expensive and perhaps ineffective treatment to a heavy drinker who refuses to give up drink.

Examiner's comment: The candidate has addressed all the requirements of the task; reasoning is coherent and convincing throughout; a readily identifiable conclusion has been reached; written communication is clear and accurate with few errors. A high Level 4 response.

Many of the activities follow worked examples, where tasks have been set and comments are provided suggesting appropriate responses. Before attempting an activity you should ensure that you have followed and understood the worked examples.

ACTIVITY 1

a) There could be a number of problems of definition, including the following:

- In the context of ASBOs, which are imposed by the courts, it might be difficult to arrive at a legal definition of the term 'respect'. Legal definitions need to be precise and specific. They have to be objective. It may prove difficult to define precisely and objectively a somewhat value-laden word like 'respect'.

- The word respect – as in 'respect agenda' and 'sense of respect' – presents us with the problem that what constitutes respect could well mean different things to different people. To the police and schools, for instance, the word might indicate respect for authority. To others, it might indicate a more general idea of recognising acceptable societal norms, such as politeness.

b) Problems of implementation arising out of problems of definition could include:

- If there cannot be a precise legal definition of the term 'respect', it follows that the courts might well find it difficult to impose appropriate sanctions on those accused of lacking 'respect'. This in turn could lead to inconsistency and even subjectivity in implementing policies, perhaps from region to region or from court to court.

- If there is no common or widely accepted definition of 'respect' and therefore of the sort of behaviour a lack of it entails, then problems with implementing policies could arise from a lack of shared values between, say, the young and the old, or between those in authority and those who are not. For a policy to be successful which is aimed at reducing anti-social behaviour in our communities – the furtherance of what Tony Blair refers to a 'respect agenda' – it needs to be based upon common understanding and consent.

ACTIVITY 2

Three factors that might affect people's views on the gender pay gap could include:

- An economic factor: Document A, from the Report of the Women and Work Commission, refers to 'this waste of talent'. The loss to the economy represented by such wasted talent could well affect the views of employers and the government concerning the pay gap. This, in turn, could lead to more effort being put in to narrow the gap in pay between men and women.

- A factor which might affect views on the gender pay gap is one connected to the moral concept of fairness. In Document B, the Director of the Fawcett Society talks about a 'generation of women being short-changed'. People might see this as being unfair and as representing an injustice that needs to be rectified. This feeling could lead to an increase in support for measures to close the pay gap.

- The views of the political parties on the gender pay gap could be affected by evidence which shows that Britain has the largest pay gaps in Europe. In Document B, for instance, George Osbourne refers to 'young mothers' and this could be an indication of a political factor at work here. Perhaps politicians will want to devise policies on equal pay in order to attract the female vote.

ACTIVITY ❸

This activity refers you to the table of ASBOs issued between 1999 and 2005. Problems that might arise in using these figures in assessing if ASBOs should continue to play a significant role in combating anti-social behaviour could include:

- The figures in themselves do not tell how effective ASBOs have been. Using the fact that over 6000 ASBOs have been issued, to argue that they should continue to be an important part of the antisocial behaviour strategy would be based upon the assumption that they have been issued because they are effective, whereas the figures do not tell us if this is the case or not. There could be other reasons why so many have been issued, such as the political desire to be seen to do something.

- Another problem with using these figures is one of context. Knowing the number of ASBOs that have been issued in each region is not, on its own, enough to enable us to make a serious and convincing case for continuing with them. We need to combine these figures with other data, such as movements in crime figures for each of the areas in the same period, particularly for the lower level disorder offences that ASBOs set out to reduce.

ACTIVITY ❹

You could probably make a case for putting each criterion in all four of the categories. There is, for instance, a case to be made that most criteria carry some sort of moral implication. The table on page 101, therefore, represents a series of suggestions rather than a prescriptive list.

Criteria	Moral	Pragmatic	Political	Economic
Environmental impact	✓	✓	✓	✓
Value for money		✓		✓
Personal freedom	✓		✓	
Equality of opportunity	✓		✓	
Community relations	✓	✓	✓	
Effects on wildlife	✓			
International norms	✓		✓	

ACTIVITY 5

Nuclear energy

- Sustainability: this is going to be a key criterion when considering future energy policy. Investment in something like nuclear energy production is likely to be very expensive, but if nuclear energy is seen as sustainable as a major source of energy over a long period then it will be seriously considered.

- Impact on the environment: this is another key criterion. The building of more nuclear power stations and the disposal of nuclear waste give rise to major environmental concerns. Any decisions about energy production must take into account environmental impact.

Smoking

- Personal freedom: in considering any move to regulate where people can and cannot smoke, we are going to come across arguments based partly at least on this issue of freedom of the individual. Smokers will claim that banning smoking, in places of entertainment for instance, is restricting their freedom, while non-smokers might claim that passive smoking is an infringement on their freedom to enjoy clean air.

- Public safety: this is another relevant criterion to apply to decisions about where people should or should not be allowed to smoke. Smoking can damage other people's health and can also be a fire risk, for example in hotel bedrooms and near flammable substances. Banning smoking in certain places can, therefore, be justified on the grounds of fulfilling the criterion of public safety.

Public demonstrations

- Public safety: this is a key criterion in deciding whether or not to allow a demonstration such as a march to take place. The authorities, such as the police and emergency services, have to be sure that crowds can be managed safely.

- Impact on community relations: this is another criterion that needs to be taken into consideration when making decisions about demonstrations. For instance, should a march be banned because it might go through an area whose community feels threatened or offended by what the marchers believe in?

ACTIVITY 6

Applying *effective use of resources* as a criterion here might be helpful because it appears to be clear, relevant and testable.

a) Usefulness of the criterion

- The police, the courts and local authorities have a lot to do; resources such as manpower, time and money have to be allocated in such a way that ensures the best value for money.

- If we can find a way of dealing with anti-social behaviour that does not involve lots of police time or form-filling then this might be an attractive choice.

- The resources that are saved by being more cost-effective can be used elsewhere, for example, in dealing with serious crimes.

- We should be able to produce some method of measuring the effective use of resources, and this will better allow us to evaluate a course of action.

b) Problems

- The general public might not be so concerned with effective use of resources as such but with the sort of actions that they can see working. This might particularly be the case in areas where anti-social behaviour is frequent.

- An effective use of resources might entail ignoring problems that are seen by the authorities as minor and which take up a lot of time when they are being dealt with. But it could be argued that anti-social behaviour is a problem because it represents an accumulation of apparently minor cases.

- An effective use of resources could involve taking actions that we might view as wrong, or at least dubious, in principle.

c) Explaining your points to others

This is the part of the activity that involves you in developing and communicating your ideas and arguments. Also you will need to be able to combine your points with those made by others in your group to present the coherent views of the group as a whole. You may need to persuade, compromise and agree to differ.

ACTIVITY ⑦

There are four choices, or options, open to you. The choice considered here is *'An outright ban on the building of new supermarkets within a 10-mile radius of smaller towns'.*

This choice has been evaluated through the application of three of the criteria: *the impact on local employment, environmental impact* **and** *public acceptability.*

The potential **impact on local employment** is going to be one of the key criteria in helping us to decide whether or not to implement such a ban. Applying this criterion, however, is likely to produce some mixed results.

The evidence provided in Document C would perhaps imply that the substantial fall in the number of independent retailers – of something like 20% – has had a negative impact on local employment in the retail sector. This, though, is based upon the assumption that the increase in the number of supermarkets is a major reason for the decline in independent retailers. This might be a reasonable assumption to make, but there could be other reasons too, such as an increase in Internet shopping or a decline in demand for some of the things supplied by smaller, more specialised retailers.

Another problem with using Document C as evidence is that it does not tell us to what extent local employment has actually been affected by the closure of smaller shops. Independent retailers are not as likely to employ the same number of people as supermarkets do. Therefore, the net effect of supermarkets on local employment might well be a positive one, with more jobs being created than lost.

However, Document B could be used to show that the kind of jobs lost when supermarkets threaten independent retailers are going to be skilled and specialised, such as pharmacists and butchers. The All-Party Parliamentary Small Shops Group (Document A) is also evidently concerned about what it sees as the 'unfair advantage' that supermarkets enjoy.

We cannot be sure, then, on the basis of the evidence we have, what the impact of banning supermarkets would have on local employment.

This shows us the importance of looking at a number of criteria. In terms of the **environmental impact** of a ban on new supermarkets within a 10-mile radius of small towns we are also likely to get some mixed results.

Document A suggests that the big supermarkets are causing some damage to the environment; their free car parks encourage more car use and new buildings take up too much floorspace. However, forcing people to drive further out of town to reach supermarkets could well lead to an adverse impact on the environment. Whilst we could argue that a 'Small Shops Group' of MPs may not be as objective as perhaps they could be, Document B says that building a new supermarket in Norwich would 'wipe out a street of local shops'. Even allowing for journalistic and personal bias in Document B, the existence of a local campaign against this supermarket plan does suggest that many local shops could be under threat. But this, in terms of environmental impact, might not be a wholly bad thing – without the shops there will be less traffic, and therefore less pollution, in the town centre. Against this argument, though, is the point that the urban landscape and environment will be less attractive with rows of closed-up shops.

Therefore, assessing the overall impact on the environment of this course of action is likely to prove problematic and to yield some contradictory findings.

In terms of **public acceptability**, the picture might, as far as Documents A and B are concerned, be a lot clearer. You might expect a group of Members of Parliament to be in tune with public opinion, and Simon Hoggart talks about 'a wave of antipathy' towards the larger supermarket chains. However, we do need to treat the views expressed in Documents A and B with some caution: they may not be typical of the mass of consumers and they may be unduly influenced by local circumstances. It might be the case that many people appear to resent the effect that the growth of supermarkets is having on their town, on employment and on the environment, while at the same time benefiting from what they see as the advantages of large supermarkets in terms of convenience, etc.

We can see then that such a course of action as a ban on new in-town supermarkets could lead to problems as well as benefits. The application of the three criteria we have selected to assess this choice has not resulted in any clear-cut answer in terms of whether such a ban ought to be put in place. However, using these criteria would help us to come to a decision based upon a careful consideration of a number of relevant factors.

ACTIVITY 8

The NHS Trust is clearly faced with a dilemma here because:

- as the body responsible for the running of the NHS in its area, the Trust has to make the decision whether or not a new and expensive drug should be freely available on prescription

- there are clearly negative consequences either way. Denying a patient free treatment could be seen as discriminatory and even cruel in terms of the pain and suffering that could result. But spending large amounts on providing an expensive, and as yet possibly unproven, treatment might result in other patients being denied treatment – on the basis that there is not an unlimited budget for drugs

- conflicting criteria could include cost versus the welfare of individual patients.

ACTIVITY 9

The magistrate has to decide whether or not to send the vicar to prison. This means sending a 70-year-old man to jail, which cannot be a good thing to do, particularly a law-abiding pillar of the community. It is also costly, as the Prison Reform Trust points out. However, if the magistrate chooses not to send the vicar to prison, s/he runs the risk of setting a bad example to other potential law-breakers, as well as being seen to have failed in their duty to uphold the law. The magistrate is faced with a dilemma.

The local council, who brought the case to court in the first place, had to make a decision: allow the vicar to get away with not paying his council tax, and risk lots of other pensioners following suit; or end up with what has happened, being held responsible for having an elderly man of the cloth put away with a bunch of criminals, and all the bad publicity that goes with it. Though it could perhaps be argued that they had no choice, as people have to pay their taxes by law, in actual fact this is not really the case as there are always some council tax arrears that have to be written off for various reasons. Therefore the local council was also faced with a dilemma.

ACTIVITY 10

Some of the comments you could have made include:

i) The statement contains two rules: 'no cans of fizzy drinks will be allowed' and 'refrain from dropping crisps and sweet wrappings anywhere on college premises'.

ii) The new policy being announced is supported by the principle – even if it may not be explicitly expressed as such – that one ought to promote a healthy lifestyle amongst those in your care.

iii) The senior management use the principle above as a reason for their decision in the sentence 'The college does apologise to all students…but we feel that we have a responsibility to promote a healthy lifestyle for our students'.

iv) There is an underlying assumption that one should lead a healthy life style. It could be concluded from this that the college should promote a healthy lifestyle.

v) There is a recommendation to students that they should choose one of the college's healthy eating options.

ACTIVITY 11

- **Economy: A good tax will bring in a lot more revenue than it costs to collect it.** The tax on petrol is part of the selling price and is forwarded to the government by the producer and the retailer. This should be a fairly streamlined and economic process.

- **Certainty: A good tax will yield in total what you have calculated.** To a car owner/road-haulier/taxi driver, etc. petrol is an essential commodity. Therefore it is unlikely that the consumption of petrol will drop all that much because of an increase in the tax. Unless the tax increases the price of petrol to above the level that people can afford to pay, the government should be able to calculate with some confidence how much they will raise from petrol taxes.

- **Ease of payment: A good tax should not be too difficult to pay or collect.** Drivers might not like paying tax on their petrol but doing so does not involve them in form-filling or anything like that. It is a simple, if not painless process, because the tax is included in the cost of the petrol.

- **Equity: A good tax should reflect people's relative ability to pay.** It could be argued that if you can afford to buy a car then you should be able to afford the petrol. However, somebody with an income of £100 a week still has to pay the same amount in tax per gallon of petrol as someone who is earning £100, 000 a week. On this basis it can be argued that the tax on petrol is unfair because it is unequal in its effects.

Verdict: a tax on petrol certainly has its merits in terms of the first three principles of taxation, though it falls down somewhat in terms of equity. (We might want to add a further comment concerning the traditional principles of taxation: it could be argued that there should be, in view of global warming, another principle of taxation – namely that a tax should, where possible, have a positive impact on the environment.)

ACTIVITY 12

The Law Lords defined three principles upon which post-divorce property settlements should be based:

- **Division of property should be determined by need:** Mrs Persimon gave up her job to try to have a family. She will need to recover at least some of that lost income from her ex-husband's assets. Mr Persimon could claim that he now has the greater need as he has a new wife and child to support. He does, however, have assets totalling £25 million.

- **Division of property needs to take into account elements of compensation:** Mrs Persimon has lost earnings of at least £280,000 during the period of her marriage. Not working for that time might also have affected her future earning power through lost opportunities for promotion and experience. However, Mr Persimon could claim that his offer of £2 million represents ample compensation.

- **Division of property should be determined by equal share:** the Law Lords stated that when a marriage ends each partner is entitled to an equal share of the assets of that partnership. They also stated that this principle is applicable as much to short marriages as to long marriages. On this basis, the ex-Mrs Persimon's claim to at least £5 million would appear to be justified in law.

Verdict: using the principles defined by the Law Lords, Mr Persimon should give his ex-wife the settlement of £5 million she is claiming. This would still leave him with enough assets to provide for the needs of his new family. It would provide the ex-Mrs Persimon with ample compensation. Mr Persimon should perhaps reflect that a strict application of the principle based upon sharing assets might well have cost him more. He should settle.

ACTIVITY 13

Child benefit should be given at the same rate for everyone.

Need: we should give to each according to their need.

Justifying the proposal:

- Children are costly to bring up and families with children do need extra resources.

- Providing child benefit on a universal basis ensures that all those who need it will receive it; it is a clear and unambiguous policy.

Opposing it:

- Well-off families not in need will receive the same amount as poorer families. A better application of this principle might be to give no child benefit to parents on higher incomes and to increase what is given to more needy families.
- There may be other groups in society who are more in need of support than families with children.

Desert: we ought to reward those in society the most who are the most deserving.

Justifying the proposal:

- Children represent the future of any society and those bringing them up deserve to be encouraged and rewarded for their efforts and sacrifices, regardless of their incomes.

Opposing it:

- It could well conflict with a principle based upon need.
- The proposal makes no distinction between responsible parents and irresponsible parents.

Right: we have a moral duty to see that all children are equally provided for.

Justifying the proposal:

- There is no risk of discrimination on the basis of family type or economic position.
- It avoids social divisions and resentments; all are seen to be being treated equally.

Opposing it:

- Universal child benefit is unlikely to ensure that children are equally provided for as such a policy does not recognise or deal with inequalities in wealth and opportunity.

Religious beliefs and values should be given precedence over secular beliefs and values.

Need

Justifying the proposal:

- Those with strong religious beliefs and values need to be able to live according to those beliefs in order to lead a good life as ordained by their faith. To deny them of this need could lead to emotional suffering, and even fear of divine punishment. Such an interpretation of need could be used to justify allowing children of different faiths to wear different dress at school.

Opposing it:

- Giving precedence to wishes or demands based upon religious beliefs and values might lead to us neglecting the needs of people who do not share those beliefs. There could, for instance, be a religious belief that the poor and needy are born that way as part of the divine order of things.

Desert

Justifying the proposal:

- We might consider that those with strong religious beliefs are more deserving of respect and consideration because such beliefs result in them leading more worthy lives. Their moral codes, for instance, might lead them to be more law-abiding and charitable.

Opposing it:

- Certain religious beliefs and values might lead to a view of desert that involves a degree of condemnation and harsh punishment which is not seen as acceptable by others.

Right

Justifying the proposal:

- It could be argued that we have a duty to abide by God's laws and the teachings of our religion. This could be viewed as a form of elitism whereby there is seen to be a moral duty to respect the rights of some people over and above those of others.

Opposing it:

- A view that religious beliefs and values should take precedence might well conflict with a more inclusive view that we should respect the rights of all citizens regardless of creed or race.

ACTIVITY ⓐ

The most likely result of applying deontological principles to this issue is that we should oppose any attempt to change the law in order to make it easier for us to help people to end their lives in the case of terminal illness. We can explain this as follows:

- Deontological principles insist that some actions are right or wrong regardless of the consequences.
- Such a principle could be that there is a duty to preserve life regardless of the consequences.
- This would include taking your own life, or helping someone to take their life.

ACTIVITY 15

Applying consequentialist principles to this issue is more likely to result in some support for a change in the law in order to make it easier for us to help people to end their lives. We can explain this as follows:

- Consequentialist principles involve weighing up the consequences – or effects – to work out the right course of action.

- Consequentialist ethics involve us in deciding on a course of action on the basis of the amount of 'goodness' produced.

- It is recognised that there are situations in which a degree of harm is unavoidable. Thus the best possible outcome is one which, in other circumstances, we might not normally choose to opt for.

- Helping a terminally ill person to die could therefore be seen to be justified, even though in general we believe that taking another life is wrong, because the amount of pain and suffering will be reduced.

ACTIVITY 16

a) The dilemma can be expressed as follows:

Should we or should we not allow the terminally ill the choice of when they should die? If we allow the terminally ill such a choice this might reduce their pain and suffering. However, such a course of action could be viewed as reducing the value we place upon human life in general, as well as perhaps placing undue pressure on the sick person. If we do not allow such a choice however, then we could be seen as denying the ill person autonomy (the right to make decisions concerning their own lives) while unnecessarily prolonging their suffering.

b) We have already seen from Activities 14 and 15 how applying deontological and consequentialist ethical principles is more than likely to lead us to different conclusions when it comes to deciding whether or not to change the law on what we can refer to as assisted suicide or voluntary euthanasia.

We do not need to repeat the points made in response to Activities 14 and 15. What we do need to do here is to see how far we might usefully employ these principles to help us to resolve our dilemma. In doing this you could make the following points:

- The conflicting outcomes resulting from the application of deontological and consequentialist ethical principles serve to highlight the difficulties inherent in such a dilemma. It will be difficult if not impossible to resolve this dilemma to the satisfaction of both sides of the argument.

- However, we can try to modify our general principles in order to fit the particular situation; we could then see how far this might help us to resolve our dilemma.

- From a consequentialist viewpoint, for instance, the act of helping a very ill person to die can be seen as justified; this is because the good achieved by reducing the suffering of the patient outweighs the harm done by ending their life. However, we might decide that the 'greater good' might be best served by **not** putting doctors or loved ones in a position where they have to agree to, or refuse, the ill person's request that their lives be ended prematurely. This might be because of the harm which could result – from abuse or misunderstandings or guilt and emotional suffering by those who have to make such a decision. It could be argued that it is for the very reasons of the greater good that we place such a high value on the preservation of life.

- It might prove more difficult to modify or adapt a deontological stance on this issue. However, what if you were to argue that it is our duty to protect people from unnecessary suffering and indignity? Or if we argued that it is our duty to respect a person's right to autonomy – our right to decide for ourselves – when it comes to decisions concerning one's own life and body? On the basis of such arguments we could perhaps conclude that the terminally ill should be allowed to choose when they are to die and who will help them to do this.

- We can see, therefore, that some modification of the general, or over-arching, principles we are applying here could help us to move closer to a resolution of our dilemma.

- However, the bottom line is that the decision we make – in this case about whether we should change the law on assisted suicide/voluntary euthanasia – will be a matter of our own judgment based upon a careful consideration of ethical principles.

It will be important for you to come to a conclusion based upon a consideration of at least two principles, about how the dilemma could be resolved. We have not provided one definitive answer here, because the conclusion you come to will depend upon the relative weight you give to each principle.

Glossary

Altruism – a consequentialist theory which asserts that it is morally good to act in a way that would lead to the greatest good for others, excluding the self

Choices – here we are referring to the different options that might be available to us when we are responding to situations where decisions need to be made. The government or other organisations might refer to these options as policies or strategies

Collective (1) – refers to situations where groups of people are affected as a whole rather than just on an individual level. **Collective decisions** are those made by, or on behalf of, society or institutions as a whole

Collective (2) – the state or any organisation we might belong to, such as school, business, family and so on

Consequentialist principles – involve weighing up the consequences to work out the right action

Credible/Credibility – whether the evidence is believable

Criteria – the plural of **criterion**, which is a standard by which something may be judged or decided. For example, *organic foodstuff must meet the criterion of being free of chemicals in its production*

Deontological principles – rules of behaviour which are claimed to be right or wrong, regardless of the consequences

Dilemma – a situation where a choice has to be made between two conflicting options, each of which will result in some undesirable consequences

Egalitarian rights theory – humans have rights in virtue of their humanity, so we all have the same rights

Egoism – a consequentialist theory which asserts that it is morally good to act in a way that would lend to the greatest good for the self

Elitist rights theory – people gain rights by virtue of social or genetic status so different people have different rights

Equity – when we refer to equity in the context of what is the right or wrong way of doing things, we are talking about issues of fairness and impartiality

Ethical principles – are general rules or guides to action which can be applied in a range of contexts and are concerned with the notion of what is morally good or bad

Ethics – theorising about what is morally good and bad

Evidence-based approach – this involves looking at evidence to help us make decisions

Hedonism – gaining pleasure and avoiding pain are what is required to achieve a good life

Hedonistic calculus – this involves using criteria to weigh up the happiness produced, for example, duration, intensity, scope, likelihood, people affected

Indicator – a measurement or means of showing the state or level of something. An indicator is used to show how an organisation is performing. For example, *the number of students gaining five or more GCSEs at grades A*–C is a good **indicator** of how well a school is performing*. An indicator might also be used to demonstrate a trend, as in *a fall in the sale of crisps might **indicate** a trend towards more healthy eating habits*

Infer/Inference – an *inference* is a conclusion reached on the basis of evidence and reasoning. In other words, it is something we have to work out from information and evidence we are given

Moral concept – an idea, or set of ideas, associated with how we should behave. For example, *fairness*

Principle – a general rule – a guide to action which can be applied beyond the immediate situation in a range of contexts

Rights – moral or legal entitlements

Significance – the weight of support given by the evidence when seen in the whole context

Index